A Just Zionism

A Just Zionism

On the Morality of the Jewish State

Chaim Gans

OXFORD
UNIVERSITY PRESS

OXFORD
UNIVERSITY PRESS

Oxford University Press, Inc., publishes works that further
Oxford University's objective of excellence
in research, scholarship, and education.

Oxford   New York
Auckland   Cape Town   Dar es Salaam   Hong Kong   Karachi
Kuala Lumpur   Madrid   Melbourne   Mexico City   Nairobi
New Delhi   Shanghai   Taipei   Toronto

With offices in
Argentina   Austria   Brazil   Chile   Czech Republic   France   Greece
Guatemala   Hungary   Italy   Japan   Poland   Portugal   Singapore
South Korea   Switzerland   Thailand   Turkey   Ukraine   Vietnam

Copyright © 2008 by Oxford University Press, Inc.

Published by Oxford University Press, Inc.
198 Madison Avenue, New York, New York 10016

www.oup.com

First published as an Oxford University Press paperback, 2011

Oxford is a registered trademark of Oxford University Press

Library of Congress Cataloging-in-Publication Data
Gans, Chaim.
A just Zionism : on the morality of the Jewish state / Chaim Gans.
p. cm.
Includes bibliographical references and index.
ISBN 978-0-19-981206-6
1. Zionism—History.   2. Jewish nationalism—History.   3. Zionism—Moral and ethical aspects.
4. Jews—Identity.   5. Israel—Politics and government.   I. Title.
DS149.G254 2008
320.54095694—dc22   2007048006

Printed in the United States of America
on acid-free paper

For Avigail and Martha

Preface

In the course of writing this book, I received aid and support from many people and institutions. Eyal Benvenisti, David Enoch, David Heyd, Alon Harel, and Andrei Marmor commented on various chapters. I presented some of the chapters at workshops for the faculty of law at Tel Aviv University. The third chapter was presented at workshops at the Law School of Northwestern University and at the Institute for Philosophy and Public Policy at the University of Maryland. The fourth chapter is based on a paper which was presented at an Israeli-Palestinian conference on the subject of Palestinian refugees held at the Max Planck Institute for International Law and Public Law in Heidelberg. After completing the book, I received invaluable comments on the whole manuscript from Charles Manekin. I am also grateful to the reviewers of the manuscript for Oxford University Press for their comments. Michal Selitarnik was, as usual, dedicated and precise in helping me to arrange the footnotes, as was Michal Kirschner, who edited my English. Michal Merling contributed last-minute research assistance for some revisions in chapter 2, and Shahar Eisner prepared the index. I am indebted to all of them.

Most of the book is written in the style of philosophical argumentation and analysis. However, I also tried to provide historical background for the practical and moral issues discussed in it. I am grateful to the historians Yosef Gorni, Yaakov Shavit, and Gideon Shimoni, who commented on this part of the book.

This book develops, modifies, and applies the general ideas elaborated in my earlier book, *The Limits of Nationalism* (Cambridge University Press, 2003), to the concrete case of Zionism and Israeli nationalism. It also discusses some issues particular to Zionism, such as the problem of the Palestinian refugees, which were not discussed at all in the previous book. Several paragraphs in the current book also appear in the previous book. Chapter 4 is based on my paper "The Palestinian Right of Return and the Justice of Zionism," *Theoretical Inquiries in Law* 5 (2004), 269. I am grateful to Cambridge University Press and to *Theoretical Inquiries in Law* for permission to use these materials.

I began working on this book in 2004 when I was a fellow in the Law and Pluralism Program at the Institute for Advanced Studies at the Hebrew University of Jerusalem. I am grateful to the director and administration of this institute as well as to my colleagues there for their support and for creating an amicable environment. I also want to thank the Cegla Center at the faculty of law at Tel Aviv University for its financial support.

Contents

A Just Zionism

Introduction

Judaism . . . seeks . . . the creation in its native land of conditions favorable to its development: a good-sized settlement of Jews working without hindrance in every branch of culture, from agriculture and handicrafts to science and literature.

—Ahad Ha'am, "The Jewish State and the Jewish Problem," 1898

Zionism was one of several Jewish nationalist ideologies prevalent among European Jews at the end of the nineteenth century.[1] Two other Jewish nationalist ideologies were those of the Bund, which was the Jewish socialist party of Lithuania, Poland, and Russia, and of the followers of the Russian-Jewish historian Shimon Dubnow. Zionism belongs to the category of ethnocultural nationalism, according to which groups sharing a common history and culture have fundamental and morally significant interests in adhering to their culture and in sustaining it for generations. Cultural nationalism holds that such interests warrant political recognition and support, primarily by the means of granting the groups in question the right to national self-determination or self-rule. The Bund and Dubnow's followers advocated cultural autonomy for the Jews in the countries where they were living.[2] The Zionist movement aspired to realize Jews' interests in

[1] The epigraph is from Hans Kohn (ed.), *Nationalism and the Jewish Ethic: Basic Writings of Ahad Ha'am* (New York: Schocken, 1962), 78. Ahad Ha'am is the pen name of essayist Asher Hirsch Ginsberg, who was one of the founders of Zionism. He regarded its political aims as an instrument for the cultural and spiritual renewal of the Jewish people.

[2] Whereas Zionism attracted Jews from both eastern and western Europe, the Bund and the *Volkspartei* influenced by Dubnow existed exclusively in eastern Europe. For more on the Bund, see Daniel Blatman, *For Our Freedom and Yours: The Jewish Labor Bund in Poland, 1939–1949* (London: Valentine Mitchell, 2003); Daniel Blatman, "The Bund: The Myth of Revolution and the Reality of Everyday Life," in Israel Bartal and Israel Guttman (eds.), *The Broken Chain: Polish Jewry through the Ages*, vol. 2 (Jerusalem: Zalman Shazar Center, 2001), 493–533 (Hebrew); Yoav Peled, *Class and Ethnicity in the Pale: The Political Economy of Jewish*

adhering to their culture and in realizing their right to self-determination in the Land of Israel rather than in places where the Jews were currently residing, or in any other territory without a special significance in the history of the Jewish people.[3] This aspiration was based on what has often been called the historical right of the Jews to the Land of Israel.[4]

Since its early days, Zionism has been the subject of an immense array of objections and criticisms. One objection was that Zionism constitutes a nationalism with a religion, rather than a nation, as its main focus. It was further argued that its goals were unattainable, that it contradicted the

---

Workers' Nationalism in Late Imperial Russia (New York: St. Martin's, 1989); Yosef Gorny, *Converging Alternatives: The Bund and the Zionist Labor Movement, 1897–1985* (Albany: State University of New York Press, 2006). In his book, Gorny also mentions the Folkists, who were inspired primarily by the historian Shimon Dubnow. Regarding the Folkists and Dubnow, see also Shmuel Dothan, *Partition of Eretz-Yisrael in the Mandatory Period: The Jewish Controversy* (Jerusalem: Yad Izhak Ben-Zvi, 1979), 29–32 (Hebrew). Regarding Dubnow's theory of autonomy, see also Gideon Shimoni, *The Zionist Ideology* (Hanover, NH: Brandeis University Press, 1995), 108–109.

[3] As indicated in the text, the Bund and Dubnow advocated Jewish autonomy in the places where Jews were living. However, there were also groups that considered establishing an autonomous political entity for the Jews in other locations. For example, the group Am Olam (Eternal People) advocated that the Jews immigrate to America and attain autonomy there (see Shimoni, *The Zionist Ideology*, 30–31). There were various territorialist groups that proposed a variety of solutions to the "problem of the Jews" (see note 4 below) and made attempts to implement them, but they should probably not be classified as national movements in the full sense of the term. Prominent examples are Baron Hirsch's attempt to found Jewish colonies in Argentina at the end of the nineteenth century (see Haim Avni, *Argentina: "The Promised Land": Baron De Hirsch's Colonization Project in the Argentine Republic* [Jerusalem: Magnes, 1973] [Hebrew]), and the establishment of the Jewish Territorial Association by a group of delegates to the Seventh Zionist Congress (1905) after the Uganda Plan had been rejected. For an account of the territorialist attempts, see Isaak Nachman Steinberg, "Territorialism: Free Israel and 'Freeland,'" in Feliks Gross and Basil J. Vlavianos (eds.), *Struggle for Tomorrow: Modern Political Ideologies of the Jewish People* (New York: Arts, Inc., 1954), 112–129; Ben Halpern, *The Idea of the Jewish State*, 2nd ed. (Cambridge, MA: Harvard University Press, 1969), 147–157; Eliahu Benjamini, *States for the Jews: Uganda, Birobidzhan and 34 Other Projects* (Tel Aviv: Hakibbutz Hameuchad, 1990) (Hebrew).

[4] The term "Land of Israel" ("Eretz Yisrael" in Hebrew) does not merely refer to the land or the territory of the State of Israel. It is the land promised to the Jewish people in the Old Testament. Jews lived and were politically dominant in many parts of it, mainly in the first millennium B.C. until the destruction of the second temple in 70 A.D. The term denotes most of the land which today comprises the State of Israel and the Kingdom of Jordan. Since the 1920s, it has mainly denoted the territories under the British Mandate—that is, the land between the Jordan River and the Mediterranean. It thus overlaps with historical Palestine. Another name for the Land of Israel in Jewish tradition (which appears frequently in the Old Testament and in liturgy) is *Zion*—also a traditional name for the holy city of Jerusalem. This of course explains why the ideology that is the subject of this book is called *Zionism*.

universalistic leanings of the Jews, and that it was impossible to reverse the dispersion of the Jewish people all over the world. There were those who claimed that "the problem of the Jews," or "the Jewish problem,"[5] would be more easily resolved by the institutionalization of their nationhood in the places where they were currently residing or by their assimilation or integration into the nations in whose midst they were living, rather than by way of their reconstitution as a distinct nation in the Land of Israel.[6] In actual practice, most of these objections to Zionist ideology were obviated or became less significant by the annihilation of European Jewry in World War II and by what could be regarded as the Zionist movement's main historical achievement, namely, the establishment of the State of Israel.[7] However, Israel's subsequent policies have given rise to a new set of objections and criticisms.

The purpose of this study is to present a philosophical analysis of the justice of contemporary Zionism as realized by the State of Israel, including Israel's territorial and demographic aspirations and the way it conceives of itself as a Jewish state. Specifically, I will examine the justice of

---

[5] In the early days of the Zionist movement, there was a debate on whether the goal of Zionism was to solve "the problem of the Jews," which meant the persecution suffered by Jewish individuals, or "the problem of Judaism." The latter referred to the continued existence of the Jews as a people.

[6] Most of the objections to Zionism came from the various sectors of the Jewish public (for example, the religious orthodoxy of central and eastern Europe, Jewish socialists in eastern Europe, and Jews in Western countries, who were attempting to assimilate into the nations where they lived) and from non-Jews, both those who were in direct conflict with Zionism (mainly the Arabs) and public figures who did not have direct contact with Zionism (such as Tolstoy and Gandhi). There are innumerable books devoted to critiques of Zionism. For a summary of the traditional critiques, see Walter Laqueur, *A History of Zionism* (New York: Schocken, 1976), chap. 8; and Halpern, *The Idea of the Jewish State*, especially chaps. 3 and 5. For criticisms of Zionism by Jews, see Haim Avni and Gideon Shimoni (eds.), *Zionism and Its Jewish Opponents* (Jerusalem: Hassifriya Haziyonit, 1990) (Hebrew).

[7] One main objection that could still be raised today, though in a somewhat weaker manner, is that Zionism constitutes a nationalism with a religion, rather than a nation, as its main focus. Despite the fact that there certainly is a Jewish *Israeli* nation in the cultural sense, many people would claim that its links with most Jews living outside Israel only pertain to religion and ethnicity, but not to culture. Moreover, there is an anomaly in Israel itself, since the role of religion is crucial in determining membership in the Jewish cultural nation. According to an Israeli Supreme Court ruling, people who are born into Jewish families, live in Israel, observe Jewish customs, feel part of the Jewish nation, but also accept Jesus as the messiah cannot be recognized as Jews under the Law of Return (HCJ 265/87, *Beresford v. The Ministry of Interior*, P.D. 43[4] 793 [Hebrew]). This certainly raises questions about the definition of the Jewish people as a nation. However, I cannot address this issue in this book.

contemporary Zionism in the light of the gap between a particular version of Zionist ideology that could be considered just and the situation today, which is a consequence of both current Israeli policies and the Zionist past. I will mainly focus on three components of this situation: the Palestinian refugee problem, which was a result of the 1948 Israeli War of Independence; the occupation of the West Bank and Gaza Strip after the 1967 Six-Day War (as well as subsequent Jewish settlement activities there); and the policies of the State of Israel toward the Arab minority living within Israel's pre-1967 borders.[8]

However, there are two types of objections to contemporary Zionism that do not focus on the aforementioned gap but rather on Zionism's defining principles. One type of objection challenges the ethnocultural principle, according to which people have a fundamental interest in adhering to their culture, in sustaining it for generations, and in receiving political recognition and support for this. The second type of objection focuses on the principle that the Jews had the right to return to the Land of Israel. Both types of objections challenge the defining principles of Zionism and therefore any possible justification for the State of Israel and its policies. I reject both of these charges against Zionism. The objection concerning the ethnocultural nature of Zionism will be the subject of chapter 1, while the arguments that question the principle calling for the return of the Jews to the Land of Israel will be discussed in chapter 2.

In present-day Israel, the right to national self-determination and self-rule is interpreted as a right to Jewish *hegemony* in a Jewish nation-state. In chapter 3, I will argue that the hegemonic interpretation of Jewish self-determination in Israel is only justified circumstantially and is only applicable to the domains of demography (by which I mean the numerical balance between the Jewish and Arab population) and security. In chapter 4, I will explicate the implications of limiting Jewish hegemony to the domains of demography and security for the arrangements between Israel and the Palestinian people *beyond* the pre-1967 borders. Specifically, I will

---

[8] Whether or not contemporary Zionism is just may also depend on numerous other facts pertaining to many specific historical situations, the complex moral issues concerning the appropriate behavior of the parties to the Arab-Israeli conflict in each of these historical contexts, and the implications of these historical facts and moral issues to the current responsibilities of the Israelis and the Arabs. I am obviously unable to undertake the Herculean task of addressing all of these issues. Moreover, I believe that it is morally incumbent upon us not to address these many complex and often controversial points at the moment in order to focus on those main issues that have thus far prevented the resolution of the Israeli-Arab conflict.

address the relationship between the justice of Zionism and the Palestinian demand for the return of Palestinian refugees to Israel, and some arguments concerning the just borders between Israel and a future Palestinian state. In chapter 5, I will explicate the implications of the limited-hegemony conception of Jewish self-determination for internal Israeli policies *within* Israel's pre-1967 borders. Specifically, I will address questions concerning the inequality between Jewish and Arab citizens of Israel, especially with regard to immigration. I will conclude this book by explaining how the implementation of a just version of Zionist ideology by Israel today would ultimately affect not only Zionism's moral standing in the present and in the future, but also the legitimacy of Israel's current reliance on the justice of Zionism in the past.

I would like to note that, for the sake of the arguments presented in this book, I will accept the Zionist narrative of Jewish history almost completely—at least those parts of it not directly involving the Zionist movement or the State of Israel. For example, I will go along with the Zionist movement's acceptance of the Judeo-Christian myth of the Jews' expulsion from the Land of Israel by the Romans, and with the role which this myth plays in the Zionist narrative of Jewish history. However, I will not accept the Zionist version of the events which led to the creation of the Palestinian refugee problem in 1948, which for the most part denies that Jewish military forces were directly involved in creating this problem. It is important to stress my acceptance of the Zionist narrative regarding those parts of Jewish history in which Zionism is not directly involved, because many details in this narrative cannot be substantiated by solid historical evidence, and also because the historiographic principle of selection according to which this narrative was constructed is ideologically biased and politically manipulated. The example just mentioned, namely, that Zionism assumes the Judeo-Christian myth that the Romans expelled the Jews from the Land of Israel, demonstrates this. There is evidence that no such expulsion ever took place.[9] Zionism accepts the myth of expulsion because expulsion, unlike abandonment, appears to provide a better justification for the Jews' return to Palestine. Zionism also takes it for granted that the Old Testament represents the true version of early Jewish history. However, there is no solid historical evidence for the truth of many of the details in the biblical story,

---

[9] See Israel J. Yuval, "The Myth of the Jewish Exile from the Land of Israel," *Common Knowledge* 12(1) (2006), 16–33.

apart from the account in the Old Testament itself. Zionism emphasizes Jewish history in biblical times because the events described in the Bible took place in Palestine, and because the Jewish people then enjoyed a unity which has been lost for thousands of years. Yet Zionism underplays Jewish history in the Middle Ages, because it occurred outside of Palestine and was fragmented into the histories of many subgroups within Judaism.

In accepting or creating various myths, and in emphasizing the importance of particular periods and historical events while on the other hand underplaying the importance of other periods and historical events, the Zionist narrative of Jewish history is not different from many narratives that other nationalist movements have constructed for their nations, nor is it different from all historical narratives.[10] Moreover, the fact that nationalist narratives are ideologically biased and include many mythical components does not constitute a sufficient reason for automatically rejecting all aspects of the nationalisms invoking these narratives.[11] The question of which particular nationalist myths or nationalist ideologies based on myths should be rejected is complex and beyond the scope of this book.[12] My main purpose here is to examine the justice of Zionism, while assuming that the Zionist reading of Jewish history is acceptable and valuable for the most part.

---

[10] Prominent sociologists and historians of nationalism, such as Ernest Renan, "Qu'est-ce qu'une nation?" in John Hutchinson and Anthony D. Smith (eds.), *Nationalism* (Oxford: Oxford University Press, 1994), 17–18; Ernest Gellner, *Nations and Nationalism* (Oxford: Basil Blackwell, 1983); Benedict Anderson, *Imagined Communities: Reflections on the Origin and Spread of Nationalism*, rev. ed. (London: Verso, 1991); and Eric J. Hobsbawm, *Nations and Nationalism since 1780*, 2nd ed. (Cambridge: Cambridge University Press, 1992), consider myth creation and historiographical manipulation to be central components of nationalism and of the concept of the modern nation. For the specific case of history construction by Zionism, see, for example, Yael Zerubavel, *Recovered Roots: Collective Memory and the Making of Israeli National Tradition* (Chicago: University of Chicago Press, 1995); Uri Ram, *The Time of the "Post": Nationalism and the Politics of Knowledge in Israel* (Tel Aviv: Resling, 2006) (Hebrew), especially chap. 1; Yitzhak Conforti, *Past Tense: Zionist Historiography and the Shaping of the National Memory* (Jerusalem: Yad Izhak Ben-Zvi, 2006) (Hebrew).

[11] For arguments concerning this claim, see David Miller, *On Nationality* (Oxford: Clarendon Press, 1995), 31–47; and Margaret Moore, *The Ethics of Nationalism* (Oxford: Oxford University Press, 2001), 9–18.

[12] Miller and Moore (ibid.) suggest some useful distinctions concerning this point. However, I do not think they exhaust the complexity of the topic.

I

Zionism as an Ethnocultural Nationalism

Historians and sociologists classify nationalist ideologies into two main types: ethnocultural nationalism and civic nationalism. According to the former type of ideology, members of groups sharing a common history and culture have fundamental, morally significant interests in adhering to their culture and in sustaining it for generations. Furthermore, these interests warrant political recognition and support, primarily by means of the right to national self-determination.[1] The ideologies of civic nationalism, by contrast, mainly argue that the citizenry of the state has an interest in sharing one homogeneous national culture. This interest is not derived from people's interest in adhering to their original culture, but rather originates because cultural homogeneity facilitates the implementation of universal values such as democracy, distributive justice, and economic growth. According to civic nationalism, when the state's citizenry's interest in cultural homogeneity conflicts with people's interest in adhering to their original culture, the former should prevail.[2] It is common among historians,

---

[1] For a detailed formulation of this interpretation of ethnocultural nationalism, see Chaim Gans, *The Limits of Nationalism* (Cambridge: Cambridge University Press, 2003), chap. 1.

[2] For the arguments in favor of this interpretation of civic nationalism, see ibid. This interpretation is based on the paradigmatic historical examples of civic nationalism, namely, the nationalisms of France and Britain, which informed the historians and sociologists who first made the distinction between civic nationalism and ethnocultural nationalism (e.g., Hans Kohn, Anthony Smith). In the nineteenth century and in the first half of the twentieth century, both France and Britain attempted to make their populations culturally homogeneous and perhaps succeeded in doing so. Some contemporary philosophers and political theorists use the term "civic nationalism" to refer to a nationalism that only centers around political principles, that is, civic principles, and the idea of a common citizenship. For criticisms of this interpretation of the concept, see Will Kymlicka, *Multicultural Citizenship: A Liberal Theory of Minority Rights* (Oxford: Clarendon, 1995), 23–24; and Gans, *The Limits of Nationalism*, 11–12. (In my view, and for reasons explained in *The Limits of Nationalism*, 15, civic nationalism ought to be called "statist nationalism." But since

sociologists, and political philosophers to conceive of ethnocultural nationalism as necessarily collectivist, illiberal, and regressive,[3] as opposed to civic nationalism, which is commonly associated with individualism, rationalism, liberalism, and progress.[4] This perspective motivated many of the objections to Zionism. However, this view of ethnocultural nationalism also underpinned numerous attempts to ascribe civic components to Zionism or to argue that it should be replaced by a civic Hebrew or Israeli nationalism. Some of the founding leaders and ideologues of Zionism did indeed espouse certain powerful core conceptions that were reminiscent of civic nationalism. In Zionist history, there have been various calls to turn it into a civic nationalism. Nonetheless, Zionism is fundamentally an ethnocultural nationalism. Accordingly, I believe that it should be interpreted as such and not be forced into categories that are alien to it. I will explain this in detail in the first section below. In sections 2 and 3 of this chapter, I will demonstrate that ethnocultural nationalism need not necessarily be illiberal and regressive. This is despite the fact that this kind of nationalism has parented numerous offshoots that are patently illiberal and unacceptable, including certain manifestations of Zionism in the past and especially in the present.

1. Zionism, Ethnoculturalism, and Civic Nationalism

A defining characteristic of ethnocultural nationalism is that the nation chronologically precedes the state that is subsequently established by that particular nation. In contrast, a defining characteristic of civic nationalism is that the state chronologically precedes the nation, which is then forged as a result of people's affiliation with this state. In that sense, Czech nationalism and Serbian nationalism are prime examples of ethnocultural nationalism. That is, they are nationalisms of groups that existed before the states subsequently established by them as means for advancing their ethnocultural interests. American nationalism and the nationalisms of France and Britain are classic examples of civic nationalism; these states existed before the

---

this term is not widely used in the current literature on nationalism, I have returned here to the more popular term for this kind of nationalism, namely, "civic nationalism.")

[3] See, e.g., Hans Kohn, *Nationalism: Its Meaning and History* (Princeton, NJ: Van Nostrand, 1955), 29–30; Michel Seymour, with the collaboration of Jocelyne Couture and Kai Nielsen, "Introduction: Questioning the Ethnic/Civic Dichotomy," in Jocelyne Couture, Kai Nielsen, and Michel Seymour (eds.), *Rethinking Nationalism* (Calgary, Alberta, Canada: University of Calgary Press, 1998), 1–61.

[4] See Seymour, Couture, and Nielsen, "Questioning the Ethnic/Civic Dichotomy," 1–9.

nations that emerged within them. They created their nations as means for implementing values such as democracy, equality, social solidarity, and cohesion among their respective citizenries. Accordingly, Zionism constitutes a clear case of ethnocultural nationalism. The original Zionist ideologues, leaders, and activists all considered themselves members of an ethnocultural group that was stateless and therefore aspired to self-determination as a means of promoting members' interests in adhering to their culture, sustaining it for generations, and protecting its members from persecution.

The claim that Zionism is fundamentally ethnocultural does not necessarily preclude acknowledging that some of the concepts expressed by Zionist ideologues and some of the processes that took place in the history of Zionism could prima facie be considered to be characteristic of civic nationalism. These concepts and processes came in a number of forms. First, some of the ideas and initiatives presented by many prominent Zionist thinkers and leaders, as well as what seemed to motivate them, are very similar to those associated with civic nationalism. Theodor Herzl, an Austro-Hungarian Jewish journalist and the founding father of Zionism, was the most prominent Zionist leader to whom this could be said to apply. But Herzl was not alone. Another such leader was Leo Pinsker, a Russian-Polish forerunner of Zionism and the author of *Autoemancipation* (1882), in which he despaired of the prospects of Jewish emancipation in Europe and called for the establishment of a Jewish homeland. Both of these men aspired to create a Jewish state, but their primary motivation was not their concern for the interests the Jews might have in adhering to their culture and in sustaining it for generations. In fact, prior to becoming Zionists, they had both advocated Jewish cultural assimilation to the majority populations of their host states, hoping that these states would eventually place less emphasis on their ethnocultural characteristics and that they would become increasingly civic. The change in their thinking, as expressed in their respective formulations of Zionism, was mainly a reaction to the persecution of Jews in Europe rather than a result of their desire to ensure the continuity of the Jews as a distinct ethnocultural group. Indeed, in their desire to found a Jewish state, they strove to implement the principles of civic nationalism rather than to establish a framework within which they could nurture and promote the ideas of ethnocultural nationalism for the preservation of Jewish culture. This is especially true of Herzl and attested to in both of his books—*The Jewish State* and *Altneuland*[5]—and by the proposal to establish

---

[5] Theodor Herzl, *The Jewish State*, trans. Sylvie d'Avigdor (New York: Dover, 1988); Theodor Herzl, *Altneuland*, trans. Lotta Levensohn (New York: Bloch, 1941).

a Jewish state in East Africa (the Uganda Plan), which he presented at the
Sixth Zionist Congress in 1903. The vision expressed in *Altneuland* reflects
Herzl's ambition to realize the universal ideas of liberalism and progress
within the framework of a Jewish state.[6] For example, Herzl envisaged German as the language of the Jewish state, rather than Hebrew or any other
Jewish language. This was only possible because Herzl's thinking seemed
to be within the conceptual framework of civic nationalism, in which language is no more than a means for promoting cultural homogeneity and
facilitating communication among citizens. Herzl did not consider language
to be a distinct component of cultural identity to which the members of
ethnocultural groups adhere precisely because they perceive it as such.[7] In
The Jewish State, Herzl argued that the Jewish people's urgent need was for a
place where they could establish that state. However, this did not necessarily
have to be the Land of Israel, as attested to by his Uganda Plan. In his view,
a specific territory for the Jews was merely a haven from persecution. He
did not consider territory to be a constituent of a people's cultural identity,
which would have to be adhered to merely because it formed a component
of their identity.[8]

---

[6] See also Anita Shapira, *Land and Power: The Zionist Resort to Force, 1881–1948*, trans.
William Templer (New York: Oxford University Press, 1992), 8; Hedva Ben-Israel, *In the Name
of the Nation: Studies in Nationalism and Zionism* (Jerusalem: Ben-Gurion University of the
Negev Press, 2004), 144 (Hebrew).

[7] Ahad Ha'am attacked *Altneuland* because of Herzl's emphasis on universal social ideas
and his neglect of Hebrew and Jewish culture. Herzl, Max Nordau (another prominent figure
in the early days of Zionism, who together with Herzl founded the World Zionist Organization), and others responded to Ahad Ha'am's critique. See Shulamit Laskov, "Altneuland,"
Zionism 15 (1990), 35–53 (Hebrew).

[8] Leo Pinsker too did not view the Land of Israel as the necessary location for the realization of Jewish nationalism: "The goal of our present endeavors must be not the 'Holy Land' but
a land of our own" (quoted in Gideon Shimoni, *The Zionist Ideology* [Hanover, NH: Brandeis
University Press, 1995], 35). Regarding Herzl's proposal at the Sixth Zionist Congress, according to which Jewish self-determination should be realized in Uganda rather than in the Land
of Israel, Shimoni contends (in the Hebrew version of his book) that "Herzl used the 'Uganda
Scheme' in an intentionally manipulative manner as a means of attaining international recognition of the Zionist cause, and not in order to relocate the Zionist goal from the Land of Israel to
eastern Africa" (Gideon Shimoni, *The Zionist Ideology*, trans. Smadar Milo [Jerusalem: Magnes,
2001], 311 [Hebrew]). Shimoni refers to a study by Isaiah Friedman on this topic: "Herzl and
the Uganda Controversy," *Iyunim Bitkumat Israel* 4 (1994), 175–203 (Hebrew). However, it must
be stressed that, even if this contention is correct, there are sufficient grounds to substantiate the
claim that Herzl's degree of commitment to the Land of Israel as the location for Jewish self-
determination was weaker than that of the eastern European Zionists. His book *The Jewish State*
and his defense of the Uganda Plan in the Sixth Zionist Congress substantiate this claim.

However, Zionism also had some characteristics of civic nationalism in view of some of the practices instituted by the State of Israel. The most prominent among them was the melting pot ideology that guided the State of Israel in its first decades and which purported to forge one homogeneous Israeli culture. The diverse Jewish communities that arrived in Israel differed from one another in language, lifestyles and customs, and their respective histories. In Israel, the Zionist movement first aspired to build a new nation, and thus, in a very important sense, the state preceded the nation. As mentioned above, one of the salient features of civic nationalism is that the state precedes the nation.

A third reason for possibly associating Zionism with civic nationalism is that the new reality created by the Zionist movement in the Land of Israel ultimately led to the emergence of various civic or quasi-civic nationalist ideologies. I refer here primarily to the Canaanite movement and Hillel Kook's Hebrew Committee of National Liberation.[9] Since the 1940s, several movements and many individuals have demanded that the State of Israel be primarily conceived as the nation-state of "Israelis," regardless of whether they are of Jewish, Arab, Druze, or any other origin.[10] The Canaanite movement wanted the state created by ethnocultural Zionism to be a stepping-stone in the formation of a new nation that would integrate all of the dwellers in the Land of Israel. One of the

---

[9] Regarding the Canaanites, see Yaakov Shavit, *The New Hebrew Nation: A Study in Israeli Heresy and Fantasy* (London: Frank Cass, 1987); James S. Diamond, *Homeland or Holy Land? The "Canaanite" Critique of Israel* (Bloomington: Indiana University Press, 1986); Boas Evron, *A National Reckoning*, 2nd ed. (Or Yehuda: Dvir, 2002) (Hebrew), chap. 15. Regarding Hillel Kook, see Shavit, *The New Hebrew Nation*, 51–73; Eran Kaplan, "A Rebel with a Cause: Hillel Kook, Begin and Jabotinsky's Ideological Legacy," *Israel Studies* 10(3) (2005), 87–103; and Joseph Agassi, *Liberal Nationalism for Israel: Towards an Israeli National Identity* (Jerusalem: Gefen, 1999).

[10] See Uri Avnery, *War or Peace in the Semitic World* (Tel Aviv: Young Palestine Association, 1947) (Hebrew). Avnery argued that the solution to the problem of the Land of Israel lay in the "evolution of a general Semitic awareness/identification that would encompass the narrow national awareness/identification of each particular nation" (ibid., 29). See also HCJ 11286/03, *Uzi Ornan et al. v. The Minister of Interior* (not published), in which a number of Israeli celebrities requested that the Interior Ministry write "Israeli" rather than "Jewish" in the space for "nationality" in their state-issued identity cards. One of their main arguments for that request originated from their desire that Israel should be similar to civic nation-states, mainly those in the West such as the United States, France, and Britain, or other nation-states, such as Turkey. The petition was signed by such prominent public figures as Uri Avnery, Shulamit Aloni, Meron Benvenisti, Professor Uzi Ornan, and Benny Peled; artists such as Joshua Sobol, S. Shifra, and Alon Olearchick; and many others. The petition was also signed by the historian Yigal Elam, who, in 1988, together with Zvi Kesseh, initiated what they referred to as the Israeli Congress, the political goal of which was similar to the one in the aforementioned petition.

movement's founding fathers advocated the eventual creation of an even larger state that would encompass and integrate most of the Levant.[11] Though inspired by the romantic idea of renewing the ancient Hebrew culture, which predated the sixth century B.C. return to Zion and the construction of the Second Temple, the Canaanite movement attempted to achieve a goal characteristic of civic nationalism, namely, founding a culturally homogeneous state.[12] Instead of regarding Israel as a center or a refuge for the Jews of the diaspora, it attempted to sever the ties with the diaspora. The other movements subscribed to less extreme versions of these ideas.[13] They contended that the bond between Israel and the Jewish diaspora should play a far less significant role than the one it actually plays in daily life in Israel and in the way the State of Israel perceives itself, and they would resort to political or legal means to sever or weaken this bond. They claimed that Israel should be regarded as the state of the nation it created—the Israeli nation—and not the state of the nation that created it, the Jewish people.[14]

However, these manifestations of civic nationalism actually attest to the depth of the ethnocultural nature of Zionism. Herzl did indeed entertain the possibility of a language other than Hebrew as the language of the Jewish state. But that possibility was never seriously considered by the Zionist movement, despite the fact that it was proposed by a leader as prominent as Herzl. This indicates that it was totally incompatible with Zionist

[11] A. G. Horon, *The Land of Kedem: A Historical and Political Guide to the Near East* (Tel Aviv: Chermon, 1970), 138 (Hebrew).

[12] Notwithstanding the strongly romantic origins and tendencies of Canaanism, this provides a firm reason to view at least certain aspects of it as characteristic of civic nationalism, for Canaanism purported to realize a plan that was essentially similar to the French state after the French Revolution: the assimilation of the disparate ethnocultural groups that dwelt in France into a nation with one culture and one citizenry.

[13] See, e.g., Agassi, *Liberal Nationalism for Israel*, whose call for the ideas of civic nationalism in Israel is made mainly by presenting Hillel Kook's ideology. On page 202, Agassi notes that when Kook conceived of his normalization plan, he proposed that all of the residents of the Mandatory Palestine be included in his plan to establish the Hebrew Republic of the Land of Israel. In his view, the non-Jewish residents of Palestine should be allowed to join the Hebrew nation if they so desired, thus becoming Hebrews for all intents and purposes. For other calls for civic nationalism in Israel or discussions of the possibility of such a nationalism in Israel, see Evron, *A National Reckoning*, 349; Shlomo Zand and Nir Baram, at http://www.nrg.co.il/online/1/ART/931/970.html (accessed 6/23/2007); Uri Ram, *The Time of the "Post": Nationalism and the Politics of Knowledge in Israel* (Tel Aviv: Resling, 2006) (Hebrew), especially chap. 4.

[14] See, for example, the petition referred to in note 10 above.

ideology.[15] The same applies to Herzl's Uganda Plan to realize Jewish self-determination in East Africa. Herzl proposed this idea at the Sixth Zionist Congress in 1903. However, its outright rejection by the Seventh Congress in 1905 attests to its fundamental unacceptability to Zionist ideology.[16] Also, the mere fact that the State of Israel was formed as a melting pot from a mélange of disparate cultural groups that had little in common does not mean that Zionism is a kind of civic nationalism. First, Israel has applied this melting pot policy to Jews only, never allowing it to be applied to members of other ethnoreligious and cultural groups residing within the state. Second, in implementing this policy, Israel has promoted the Jews' interests in uniting with their cultural group and sustaining it for generations. It did not purport to use the melting pot policy in order to facilitate the realization of universal values, such as democracy and distributive justice for its entire population.

With regard to the fact that Zionism featured individuals and movements espousing civic nationalism, the following should be noted: The leaders of these movements were shaped in large part by Zionism.[17] To

---

[15] Herzl's Zionism was a response to anti-Semitism. He had originally attempted to assimilate into the nation in whose midst he dwelled and had actually regarded assimilation as the appropriate path for the Jews to take. However, this option was thwarted by rampant anti-Semitism. Herzl did not view the Jews as having a primary interest in adhering to their culture and in sustaining it for generations. He regarded the establishment of a Jewish state not as a primary interest, but rather as a remedy for damage experienced. Specifically, this interest did not precede persecution and anti-Semitism, but was produced by persecution and anti-Semitism. However, the Zionists of Eastern Europe were motivated by a different set of beliefs, namely, by what they regarded as the Jews' fundamental interest in adhering to their culture and ensuring its multigenerational survival. In contrast to Herzl, they viewed anti-Semitism as a catalyst for Jewish awareness of the urgency of taking control of their primary interests, and not as the reason or justification for the emergence of these interests. These assumptions became defining components of the Zionist ethos. See Shapira, *Land and Power*, 7–8. This is attested to by the fact that Ahad Ha'am's critique of Herzl's *Altneuland* prompted Herzl to apologetically retreat from his proposal that Hebrew should not be the official language of the Jewish state. It was Nordau who actually voiced this change on Herzl's behalf. Regarding the response to Ahad Ha'am's criticism of *Altneuland*, see Laskov, "Altneuland."

[16] It should also be noted here that, in view of unbridled criticism, Herzl himself was forced to present his Uganda Plan in an apologetic manner, describing it as a plan for a temporary "night refuge" for the Jews. This refuge seemed crucial in the wake of the Kishnev pogrom (which took place in Kishnev, Russia, at Easter in 1903, and in which dozens of Jews were killed) and Herzl's diplomatic failure in procuring a charter for the Land of Israel. Herzl's presentation of the Uganda Plan as a night refuge is discussed in Ben Halpern, *The Idea of the Jewish State*, 2nd ed. (Cambridge, MA: Harvard University Press, 1969), 154.

[17] See note 10 above.

some extent, the leadership of these groups was committed to the main principles of Zionism and had motives very similar to those of Zionism itself. However, the movements in question have in actuality always tried to supplant Zionism. The claim that they branched off from Zionism does not make Zionism a type of civic nationalism. Indeed, it is akin to claiming that Christianity's emergence from Judaism imbued Judaism with shades of Christianity. At any rate, even if the attempts to portray Zionism as an ideology that belongs to civic nationalism or to transform it accordingly are not altogether groundless, this book focuses primarily on the justifications of Zionism and its limits as an ethnocultural ideology and movement.[18]

2. "Bad" Nationalisms and "Good" Nationalisms

One of the primary factors giving rise to the civic nationalist position within Zionism—and partly why some Israelis identify with the civic aspects of Herzl's writings—is the bad reputation acquired by ethnocultural nationalism in the first half of the twentieth century. In making the distinction between these two types of nationalism, historians and sociologists have combined geographical, sociological, judgmental, and normative parameters. The historian Hans Kohn, who was the first to make this distinction after World War II, characterized territorial-civic nationalism as Western and ethnocultural nationalism as Eastern. The former involves a strong middle class, whereas the latter involves intellectuals operating in a society that has either a weak middle class or no middle class at all. However, he mainly characterized civic nationalism as progressive and as inspired by the legal and rational concept of citizenship, as opposed to ethnocultural nationalism, which he characterized as regressive and inspired by emotions and by the unconscious development of the *Volk* and its primordial and

---

[18] However, it should not be concluded that I am against urging Israel to develop a civic nationalism in the sense this term is used among some contemporary writers (see note 2 above), namely, a so-called nationalism that only centers around political and civic principles. However, the desirability of developing such nationalism in Israel does not mean that the interests of the Jews and the Arabs in Israel in adhering to their original cultures and in living substantial parts of their lives within them should be ignored. Zionism was largely a response to the Jews' interests in maintaining their culture and living within it. This book concentrates on Zionism and on what Israel can legitimately do in order to implement it as an ethnocultural nationalism. There is much to be said on what Israel should do in order to create solidarity and cohesion among all its current Jewish and Arab citizens. However, this is not the major concern of the current book.

atavistic *spirit*.[19] Moreover, at least until recently, the prevalent view has been that cultural nationalism can only emerge from collectivist antihumanistic ideologies. Cultural nationalism is sometimes considered to be synonymous with such ideologies, or at least to be their natural mate. It has been widely believed that civic nationalism is necessarily liberal and that it is the only possible form of liberal nationalism.[20] If these views are correct, then they would necessarily provide liberals with reasons for rejecting Zionism.

However, these views are wrong both in terms of the possible justifications of the basic tenets of civic and ethnocultural nationalism and in terms of the concrete historical phenomenology of each of these families of nationalism. As stated above, the basic tenet of civic nationalism is that states have an interest in their populations being nationally and culturally homogeneous. But this tenet could be and has been endorsed for reasons stemming from divergent kinds of values and political goals. Mill claimed that national and cultural homogeneity was necessary for the maintenance of a representative government.[21] Marx argued that this kind of homogeneity was necessary for the emergence of an advanced form of capitalism that was itself a precondition for a proletarian revolution.[22] Conservative thinkers could contend that the cultural unity of the state's population was necessary for the preservation of social and political stability. Clearly, civic nationalism is based on an instrumentalist rationale, according to which national cultural unity is no more than a means for the realization of important political goals. As such, it is flexible and adaptable to values both to the left and to the right of liberalism.

Furthermore, the actual history of civic nationalism also includes illiberal acts, even though some of the goals of these acts were liberal. Nation-building processes have frequently involved forced conversions of identity and other manifestly illiberal measures. This is true not only of nations such as Turkey, which, until recently, attempted to forcibly assimilate its Kurdish minority, but also of states such as France, Britain, and Australia. In Australia, until the 1960s, young Aboriginal girls were kidnapped from their families

---

[19] Kohn, *Nationalism: Its Meaning and History*, 29–30.

[20] See, e.g., Michael Ignatieff, *Blood and Belonging: Journeys into the New Nationalism* (New York: Noonday, 1993), 6; William Pfaff, *The Wrath of Nations: Civilization and the Furies of Nationalism* (New York: Simon & Schuster, 1993).

[21] John Stuart Mill, "Representative Government," in John Stuart Mill, *Utilitarianism; On Liberty; Considerations on Representative Government; Remarks on Bentham's Philosophy*, ed. Geraint Williams (London: Dent, 1993), chap. 16.

[22] Ephraim Nimni, *Marxism and Nationalism* (London: Pluto, 1991), 17–43.

in order to obliterate their original identities and to assimilate them into the culture of the majority, which was primarily of European origin. France attempted to turn the Bretons and the Provençals into Frenchmen by prohibiting them from speaking Breton and Provençal, respectively. Until the 1940s, Britain adopted a similar practice in Wales.[23]

As I have stated, the fundamental tenet of ethnocultural nationalism is that people have an interest in adhering to their culture and in sustaining it for generations, and these interests warrant state support. Contrary to the view that such nationalism must necessarily be identified with antihumanist and antiliberal ideologies, this tenet has actually been derived from a broader range of values, political goals, and philosophical presuppositions. Some ethnocultural nationalist thinkers are indeed collectivists who believe that people's interest in adhering to their culture stems from the fact that they are no more than a cell in the organism of their nation, or a fish in the nation's aquarium, and that they therefore cannot exist without their nation. They believe that the nation precedes its human components both ontologically, in terms of their existence as individuals, and morally, in terms of their value.[24] However, there are ethnocultural nationalists who are individualists. They believe that many individuals have interests in adhering to their culture and in sustaining it for generations because their culture constitutes an important component of their identity, because it constitutes the world where their endeavors will leave their mark, and because to a large extent their welfare depends on whether or not their culture flourishes.[25] These interpretations of people's interests in adhering to their culture and sustaining it for generations do not presuppose collectivism.

[23] For a detailed discussion of these matters, see Gans, *The Limits of Nationalism*, chap. 1, esp. 17–20. Perhaps it is worthwhile to note here that Canaanism had also entertained the idea of forcibly assimilating some of the Oriental peoples into the Hebrew nation. See Shavit, *The New Hebrew Nation*, 85–87; Evron, *A National Reckoning*, 343–344; Diamond, *Homeland or Holy Land?* 65–68.

[24] For a more detailed and nuanced characterization of the precedence of nations over their individual members according to collectivist versions of ethnocultural nationalism, see Isaiah Berlin, "Nationalism: Past Neglect and Present Power," in his *Against the Current: Essays in the History of Ideas*, ed. Henry Hardy (New York: Viking, 1980), 333–355, especially 341–343. See also Brian Barry, *Culture and Equality: An Egalitarian Critique of Multiculturalism* (Cambridge: Polity, 2001), 11, 260–265.

[25] See, for example, Kymlicka, *Multicultural Citizenship*; Joseph Raz and Avishai Margalit, "National Self-Determination," in Joseph Raz, *Ethics in the Public Domain: Essays in the Morality of Law and Politics*, rev. ed. (Oxford: Clarendon, 1994), 125–145; Charles Taylor, "The Politics of Recognition," in A. Gutmann (ed.), *Multiculturalism: Examining the Politics of Recognition* (Princeton, NJ: Princeton University Press, 1994), 25–73; Gans, *The Limits of Nationalism*, chap. 2.

The bottom line of all this is, therefore, that just as civic nationalism can be endorsed for both liberal and nonliberal reasons, so too can ethnocultural nationalism be endorsed for both of these kinds of reasons. Moreover, in the same way that the historical realizations of civic nationalism can be said to have been both liberal and illiberal, the historical realizations of ethnocultural nationalism also have had this dual nature. Many scholars of nationalism have noted this. They stress the fact that acts of genocide and population transfers have indeed been performed in the name of ethnocultural nationalism, but that, for many groups, this form of nationalism has also paved their way from serfdom to freedom.[26] The reasoning according to which Zionism must be rejected just because it is a nationalism of the ethnocultural type, because this type of nationalism is necessarily anti-individualist and antiliberal, or because the history of this type of nationalism is irredeemably evil, is therefore a fallacious one. It is similarly wrong to argue that ethnocultural Zionism ought to be replaced by Israeli civic nationalism just because the philosophical presuppositions of civic nationalism are necessarily humanistic and liberal and because its history is wholly laudable, whereas the philosophical presuppositions of cultural nationalism are necessarily illiberal and its history totally abhorrent.[27]

The ethnocultural nationalism of a given group could be morally acceptable if two conditions obtain. First, its demands must reflect equal consideration of similar demands made by other nations. Second, it must be based on the interests of the individuals belonging to the group who wish to live within the group's culture and to sustain it for generations. It must presuppose a moral precedence of those individuals over the group. These two

[26] Yael Tamir, *Liberal Nationalism* (Princeton, NJ: Princeton University Press, 1993), 4.

[27] One might argue that forced assimilation, which was actually practiced by the historical movements of civic nationalism, does not necessarily follow from the ideology of civic nationalism, and therefore, the ideology remains intact despite its historical realizations. The response to this argument is, first, that if this contention is true, then a similar contention is also true with regard to ethnocultural nationalism. The latter is commonly accused of ugly and even criminal historical manifestations. However, it could be argued that these historical manifestations of cultural nationalism are not necessary consequences of the implementation of this ideology. Second, it is doubtful whether, given the geodemographic conditions of the world, it could seriously be maintained that the practice of forced assimilation is not a necessary consequence of the ideology of civic nationalism. A strong civic nationalism of the sort that was prevalent in France and Britain during the nineteenth century and the first half of the twentieth century has a propensity for using assimilation as a technique for attaining cultural homogeneity. Relinquishing assimilation in favor of creating a nested cultural identity (for example, as in Britain) means moving from the ideology of civic nationalism to a multicultural ideology (though not necessarily a strong version of this ideology).

conditions constitute the basis of my discussion of what was appropriate for Zionism in the past and what its policies should be today. Of course, with regard to the individual interests that justified Zionism, we cannot confine ourselves only to their ordinary interest in self-determination. We must also consider the more urgent interest that characterized the Jewish experience from the second half of the nineteenth century until the first half of the twentieth century, namely, the need to escape persecution, humiliation, and physical danger. The fact that the persecution of Jews has motivated some people to suggest collectivist, religious, and ultranationalist interpretations of Zionism does not entail a rejection of the possibility of secular, equality-based interpretations of Zionism that derive from individual interests. Quite the contrary, the interest of Jews in escaping persecution and protecting their dignity is essentially an individual interest. The fact that it motivated Zionism in its early days provides both historical and moral support for an individualistic and liberal interpretation of Zionism.

As an ethnocultural ideology, however, Zionism is not only exposed to liberal objections if ethnocultural nationalism is necessarily interpreted as collectivist and chauvinistic. According to certain interpretations of liberalism—for example, a cosmopolitan interpretation—even noncollectivist and nonchauvinistic versions of ethnocultural nationalism could be rejected. Cosmopolitan liberalism denies the contention that people have a real interest in adhering to their culture and in sustaining it for generations. Another form of liberalism which would reject ethnocultural nationalism is neutralist liberalism, which does not deny the contention that people might have an interest in adhering to their culture and in preserving it for generations, but rather rejects the claim that it is the business of the state to support these interests. Of course, these possible liberal rejections of Zionism are applicable not only to Zionism, but to all ethnocultural nationalist ideologies as such. They are discussed extensively by contemporary political philosophers in the literature dealing with multiculturalism and nationalism. In order to make a complete case for the tenability of some possible versions of Zionism, I will now present a summary of these arguments and their rebuttals.

3. COSMOPOLITAN AND NEUTRALIST OBJECTIONS TO NATIONALISM

According to cosmopolitan liberalism, even if many people do actually wish to adhere to their culture and to sustain it for generations, these desires cannot be regarded as fundamental interests. First, some people do not have such desires and are quite happy to live without maintaining contact with their original cultures. Second, people's lives might be better and more fulfilling if they were to relinquish their adherence to their original cultures. People should therefore glean a new culture from a variety of cultural traditions, conducting their lives in constant oscillation between these traditions. Moreover, it is argued that, in our postmodern world, this is not only desirable, but actually necessary. Consequently, ethnocultural nationalism (and perhaps even civic nationalism) should not be encouraged; there is certainly no justification for creating a political environment which facilitates cultural nationalism (and perhaps there is also no justification for creating a political environment which facilitates civic nationalism). The world political order ought to be arranged so that it encourages people to desist from their dependence on their original culture. It ought to encourage them to nurture cultural mobility and versatility.[28]

One response to the cosmopolitan argument is to deny that it is valid to infer the viability of the cosmopolitan alternative from the fact that happy cosmopolitans do indeed exist. Arguing for the viability of the cosmopolitan alternative just because there are some cosmopolitans who are happy would be tantamount to arguing that since there are some happy monks, celibacy is a real option for most people.[29] There are opponents of cosmopolitanism who would argue that, in view of the attributes of human nature, the well-being of most people depends on their being able to live their lives within the framework of the particular culture in which they were raised. However, a response to cosmopolitanism could hinge on a weaker premise, which makes no claims regarding human nature. According to this weaker rejection of cosmopolitanism, most people living *today* are connected to their cultures by ties that cannot be severed without causing them intense suffering. For most people today, their culture is a central component of their identity, and their affiliation with their culture is important for their well-being. As such, it is immaterial if the cosmopolitan option is ideally better for people than the nationalist one; there is no justification for interfering with their desire to adhere to their original culture, any more than there is any justification for interfering in the decisions people make

---

[28] This liberal-cosmopolitan argument is Jeremy Waldron's. See Waldron, "Minority Cultures and the Cosmopolitan Alternative," *University of Michigan Journal of Law Reform* 25 (1991–1992), 751–793.

[29] This is Kymlicka's response to Waldron's cosmopolitan argument. See Kymlicka, *Multicultural Citizenship*, 85–86.

in choosing a spouse, even if their ultimate choice may not be the very best one for them. As long as people ascribe importance to their cultural affiliations, the political environment should be structured to allow them to adhere to and to sustain their cultures. On the other hand, it should not be structured in such a way that would prevent them from relinquishing their cultures, if they so desire. I prefer the weaker response to the cosmopolitan argument, which does not hinge on a claim regarding human nature, but rather on the empirical claim that many and perhaps most people living today are strongly connected to specific ethnocultural groups.[30]

In contrast to cosmopolitan liberalism, neutralist liberalism does not deny that people have an interest in adhering to their cultures. It only opposes state interference in favor of one ethnocultural group (or several ethnocultural groups). According to this conception of liberalism, just as the state should be neutral with respect to all religions, the state should neither be identified nor associated with any particular ethnicities or cultures.[31] A number of writers have already noted that states cannot be neutral with respect to their support of culture in the same way as they can perhaps be neutral with respect to religion. The reason is that it is impossible to avoid giving preference to a particular language or particular languages spoken by their citizens. Preferring certain languages over others is an unavoidable practical necessity. As a result, in a multiethnic and multinational state, the state cannot be neutral with regard to its citizens' interests in adhering to their original languages and cultures. In actual practice, the state's choice of one particular language over other languages means demonstrating preference for the cultural group that speaks that language. The fact that their language has been chosen makes it possible for members of that group to adhere to their culture and to sustain it for generations, while the same possibilities are denied to other citizens.

On the practical level, there is no way out of this predicament. The ideal that states should be neutral in the cultural sense is therefore necessarily unattainable, and it has not and cannot be implemented by any state. In this context, Will Kymlicka noted the language policy implemented by the United States, which is "the allegedly prototypically 'neutral' state." In the United States, there is a legal requirement for children to learn English in schools. Knowledge of English is a condition imposed on immigrants for

---

[30] For a detailed discussion, see Gans, *The Limits of Nationalism*, 45–46, 160–165.

[31] For a statement of the neutralist argument see Barry, *Culture and Equality*, 27–30, 64–68, and many other places in Barry's book.

receiving citizenship, and it is also a condition for employment in government. Kymlicka further noted that the borders of the states in the United States and the dates on which new states joined the Union were intentionally determined in a manner that would ensure an English-speaking majority in these states. According to him, these requirements and decisions "have played a central role in determining which ethno-lingual groups would thrive and which would diminish."[32]

In the light of these arguments, it seems that one must reject the claim that a liberal ethnocultural nationalism is not possible. One must therefore also reject the position of those who object to Zionism just because it is an ethnocultural nationalism. Nonetheless, this does not mean that ethnocultural nationalisms cannot have versions that are susceptible to even graver objections. As I argued earlier, ethnocultural nationalism is one of two categories of nationalist ideologies. Each of these categories of ideologies could have and in fact has had various offshoots that differ widely from one another. Cultural nationalism has had a variety of forms. Inter alia, these include liberal and fascist, socialist and conservative, humanist and antihumanist versions as well as chauvinist and egalitarian, collectivist and individualistic, ethnocentric and non-ethnocentric, state-seeking and non-state-seeking forms of nationalism. Just as ethnocultural nationalism has come in all of these forms, so too has Zionism.

My intention thus far has been to demonstrate that Zionism should not be rejected just because it is an ethnocultural ideology. However, this does not mean that all versions of Zionism should be accepted. In this book, I will not discuss those forms of Zionism which I find morally repugnant. Examples of such objectionable ideologies are collectivist versions of Zionism that elevate the value of the Jewish collective over the individuals comprising it, and ethnocentric and chauvinistic ideologies, which posit the existence of a Jewish nation as a value that necessarily prevails over all other values. My aim in this book is to explore a just version of Zionism as a liberal ethnocultural nationalism. Such an ideology would ascribe value to the Jewish collective because of the importance which its individual members ascribe to it. In this form of Zionism, the Jewish nation would be regarded as equal to all other nations. Moreover, such Zionism would not consider the value of the nation as the only value that individuals ought to pursue,

---

[32] Will Kymlicka, "Western Political Theory and Ethnic Relations in Eastern Europe," in Will Kymlicka and Magda Opalski (eds.), *Can Liberal Pluralism Be Exported? Western Political Theory and Ethnic Relations in Eastern Europe* (Oxford: Oxford University Press, 2001), 13–106, 17.

but rather as one that competes with other humanistic values, such as equality or freedom. If Zionism is interpreted in this way, there is no reason to reject it just because it is a nationalist ideology of the ethnocultural type.

While Zionism is a Jewish version of ethnocultural nationalism, it differed initially from other Jewish and non-Jewish ethnocultural ideologies by virtue of its aspiration to realize the nationalist ambitions of the group it represents not in the places in which the members of this group were currently living, but rather in the historical homeland from which the Jewish people had been cut off since antiquity. Since the inception of Zionism, this homeland was and continues to be the homeland of another ethnocultural group. In spite of this, the Zionist movement resorted to the historical rights argument to justify the Jewish return to the Land of Israel. I will now address the question of whether this argument could justify the Zionist aspiration for the Jewish return to the Land of Israel under these particular conditions.

2

The Jews' Return to the
Historical Homeland

In this chapter, I will argue that historical rights constituted a significant moral consideration in favor of establishing Jewish self-determination in Palestine. However, I will also argue that were it not for the fact that Jews had been victims of persecution in the years 1880–1945, it would have been unacceptable for them to act upon this consideration. Due to this persecution many Jews, some of whom became central figures in the Zionist movement, adopted the idea of the Jewish return to Palestine.[1] I will argue that the historical rights argument, in conjunction with the horrendous scope and nature of the persecution in the 1930s and 1940s, provided justification for establishing Jewish self-determination in the Land of Israel.

However, I will also argue that there were significant justifications for the Arabs' opposition to Jews' return to the Land of Israel. The main reasons justifying their opposition derive from the fact that the Zionist movement frequently deviated from those aspirations that were justifiable. I shall not discuss these deviations in this chapter. Instead, I will argue that, to a certain extent, the Arab opposition to Zionism was justifiable even if the Zionist movement had not exceeded its justified aspirations. The complex and exceptional combination of principles and circumstances which have sustained Zionism since its inception can be invoked to explain why the Arabs were also justified in opposing it.

[1] Among the central figures of the Zionist movement for whom the persecution of the Jews was a significant reason for adopting the idea of the Jewish return to the Land of Israel are early figures such as Pinsker and Herzl and later leaders such as David Ben-Gurion (a major Zionist leader in the first half of the twentieth century who later became the first prime minister of Israel), Ze'ev Jabotinsky (the founder of the right-wing Revisionist faction within Zionism), and Chaim Weizmann (a leading statesman in Zionism's formative years who was later elected the first president of the State of Israel).

1. Interpretations of Historical Rights

It must be stressed that it is not merely the recourse to the historical rights argument which distinguishes Zionism from other ethnocultural nationalisms. Bismarck also invoked this argument in order to justify the annexation of Alsace-Lorraine to Germany in 1870. Thomas Masaryk used it in order to justify the inclusion of the Sudetenland in Czechoslovakia after World War I, and Slobodan Milosevic recently employed historical rights to justify the expulsion of the Albanians from Kosovo. However, there are two significant differences between the possible interpretations of the early Zionist use of this argument and how the notion of historical rights could be interpreted in the cases just mentioned and in many additional cases. First, Zionism could be regarded as having invoked the historical rights argument primarily in order to stress *the primacy of the Land of Israel in the history of the Jews* (henceforth, the formative territory claim). On the other hand, those who invoked it in most other cases referred mainly to *the primacy of the nations they represented in the history of the territories they were claiming* (henceforth, the first occupancy claim).[2] Second, while Zionism could be interpreted as resorting to the historical rights argument as *a consideration for selecting the geographical site for the realization of the right to Jewish self-determination*, the majority of the other cases involves nations that were already living in their historical homelands and were already enjoying (or were about to enjoy) the benefits of the right to national self-determination therein. In these

---

[2] In this sense, the Serbian refusal to allow Albanian autonomy in Kosovo, and perhaps many instances of native nations demanding to return to their homelands in "New World" countries such as America, Australia, and New Zealand, bear a certain resemblance to the Jews' claim to the Land of Israel. The current discussion of historical rights and their force as grounds for sovereignty or other territorial rights pertaining to self-determination is a concise summary of my far more extensive discussion in chapter 4 of my book *The Limits of Nationalism* (Cambridge: Cambridge University Press, 2003), which was based on Gans, "Historical Rights," *Mishpatim* 21 (1992), 193–220 (Hebrew). The distinctions between historical rights as referring to the primacy of a given nation in a given territory (the right of first occupancy) and historical rights as referring to the primacy of a given territory in the history of a given nation (the right to formative territory), and the distinction between historical rights as grounds for the very right to territorial sovereignty and historical rights as grounds for selecting the site of self-determination are central to this discussion. A distinction similar to the distinction between the right of first occupancy and the right to formative territories can be found in Reuven Gafni (Weinshenker), *Our Historical-Legal Right to Eretz Israel* (Jerusalem: Sifriyat Torah ve-Avoda, 1933) (Hebrew); and Joseph Heller, *The Zionist Idea* (London: Joint Zionist Publications Committee, 1947), 64–67. Regarding these essays, see Gideon Shimoni, *The Zionist Ideology* (Hanover, NH: Brandeis University Press, 1995), 355–357.

cases, the historical rights argument was invoked *in order to justify demands for territorial expansion.* In resorting to historical rights as a justification for such demands, one necessarily presupposes that historical rights constitute a basis for the right to territorial sovereignty and the size of the territory in question. Thus, one cannot assume that historical rights are *merely* a basis for selecting the geographical site for the realization of the right to national self-determination.

It is important to distinguish between the issue of selecting the geographical site of the right to national self-determination, on the one hand, and, on the other hand, the issue of justifying the right itself, its institutional form, and its territorial scope. Unlike historical rights, which are acquired by virtue of specific events in which the specific claimant to such rights was involved, the right to self-determination could be said to be ahistorical. Groups are entitled to it by virtue of belonging to a general category (namely, a nation) and not by virtue of any particular events in their history.[3] If historical rights alone constitute the justification for the right to territorial sovereignty, then they also provide the answers to questions concerning the appropriate geographical site, territorial scope, and institutional form of the right to national self-determination. If historical rights give rise to territorial sovereignty, they necessarily presuppose a statist realization of self-determination that applies to all of the area that has been claimed. On the other hand, justifying the ahistorical right to national self-determination by means, for example, of the argument that it allows individuals to live their lives within the framework of their culture, does not predetermine what the appropriate institutional framework of such self-determination should be (for example, personal autonomy in various spheres of life, territorial autonomy, or sovereignty in the framework of a nation-state), what its territorial scope ought to be, or where the appropriate geographical site for the realization of this self-determination should be. Historical rights could constitute a solution to this third problem concerning the site of the territory designated for self-determination, without necessarily determining its institutional character and the scope of the territories in which self-determination is realized.[4]

---

[3] Compare this to the analogous distinction between special and general rights: H. L. A Hart, "Are There Any Natural Rights?" in Jeremy Waldron (ed.), *Theories of Rights* (New York: Oxford University Press, 1984), 77–90.

[4] For a more detailed discussion of the right to self-determination and its interpretations, see chapter 3, section 1.

Like the other kinds of Jewish ethnocultural nationalism at the end of the nineteenth century, the Zionist movement conceived of the Jewish right to self-determination as an ahistorical and universal right that Jews have in the same way that other peoples do. It was the fact that the Jews had not realized the right to self-determination, in conjunction with the persecution that they suffered and with the failure of their attempts to integrate with the nations among which they lived, that gave rise to Zionism and to the other kinds of Jewish nationalisms at the end of the nineteenth century. These Jewish nationalisms were surely not driven by mere territorial ambitions.[5] The dispute between Zionism and the other Jewish ethnocultural nationalisms was primarily with regard to the geographical location where Jewish self-determination should be realized. There were at least three views on this issue: One was that of the Bund's and Dubnow's followers, namely, that the Jews should realize their self-determination nonterritorially where they were currently living in eastern and central Europe. The territorialists, who seceded from the Zionist movement, had another view: that Jewish self-determination should be realized territorially in other territories, such as Uganda. The third view was that of the "Zion's Zionists," also called "Palestinians" at the time. By invoking the historical rights argument, they claimed that Jewish self-determination should be realized in Palestine. This approach ultimately became the exclusive and defining position of Zionism following the debate with the territorialists in the Sixth and Seventh Zionist Congresses (1903 and 1905, respectively).

Zionism did indeed provide one of the answers to the question of where to realize Jewish self-determination. However, the Zionist movement's employment of the historical rights argument does not mean that all Zionist leaders and thinkers viewed this argument as simply a way to settle on the geographical site of Jewish self-determination. Many Zionist leaders and thinkers failed to distinguish between historical rights as merely a consideration for selecting the site of self-determination and as the basis for territorial sovereignty. Thus, many of them spoke of the historical rights as rights to the Land of Israel, clearly implying a claim of sovereignty over this *entire* territory.[6] However, there were also those who seemed to have

---

[5] This does not mean that the first Zionists did not invoke colonialist arguments in order to mobilize support from the great powers for their cause. Both Herzl and others resorted to such arguments. See Shimoni, *The Zionist Ideology*, 351–352.

[6] In 1882, Moses Leib Lilienblum wrote: "We have an historical right [to Eretz Yisrael] which has neither lapsed nor been forfeited with the loss of our sovereignty, just as the right of the Balkan nations to their lands has not lapsed with the loss of their sovereignty" (quoted in Shimoni, *The Zionist Ideology*, 351).

recognized that it was possible to use historical rights merely as a consideration for selecting the site of Jewish self-determination. They referred to historical rights as rights *within* the Land of Israel and not to the entire territory. Not surprisingly, Ahad Ha'am, one of the founders of Zionism, who regarded its political aims as an instrument for the cultural and spiritual renewal of the Jewish people, seemed to have recognized this.[7] However, the idea that historical rights referred to rights within the Land of Israel and not to the entire territory can also be found in many important Zionist documents. For instance, in the Basel Program, which was decided on by the First Zionist Congress, Zionism was defined as "striv[ing] to create for the Jewish people a home *in* Palestine" (italics mine).[8] The Balfour Declaration[9] speaks of the constitution of a national home *in* the Land of Israel.[10] Another important Zionist declaration that should be mentioned in this

---

[7] In "Three Steps," he states: "[B]ut there is one national right...that we will also constitute the 'majority' in one country under the sun, one land *in* which our historical right is undisputed" (italics mine; *The Writings of Ahad Ha'am* [Tel Aviv: Dvir, 1947], 153 [Hebrew]).

[8] Quoted in Shimoni, *The Zionist Ideology*, 352.

[9] The Balfour Declaration, which Chaim Weizmann succeeded in convincing the British government to issue, stated that the British government supported Zionist plans for a Jewish "national home" in Palestine. The Balfour Declaration was granted to the Zionist movement on November 2, 1917, in the form of a letter from the British foreign secretary, Arthur James Balfour, to Lord Rothschild, who was a prominent figure in the British Jewish community.

[10] As is ordinarily the case in the drafting of political documents, both the Basel Program and the Balfour Declaration were the end products of a process of balancing and making compromises among divergent considerations and constraints. Max Bodenheimer was one of the authors of the Basel Program, which was presented at the First Zionist Congress in 1897. In objecting to the 1937 plan to partition Palestine as recommended by the British appointed Royal Commission headed by Lord Peel, he explained that political Zionism strove for a state in the entire country. The Basel Program's reference to a safe haven for the Jews in the Land of Israel and the fact that it did not mention the idea of a state in the entire country were motivated by the understanding that Zionism could not push for its ultimate goals at such an early stage and that it was preferable to wait until there was a Jewish majority in the entire country. See Shmuel Dothan, *Partition of Eretz-Israel in the Mandatory Period: The Jewish Controversy* (Jerusalem: Yad Izhak Ben-Zvi, 1979), 97 (Hebrew); and Ben Halpern, *The Idea of the Jewish State*, 2nd ed. (Cambridge, MA: Harvard University Press, 1969), 30, on the considerations that motivated Herzl to propose the version of the Basel Program that was adopted by the Zionist Congress. One of the drafts that preceded the final version of the Balfour Declaration did not refer to the establishment of a national home for the Jews in Palestine, but rather to the "reconstitution" of Palestine "as a national home for the Jewish people." It was only the pressure exerted by one of the British foreign office officials which produced the transition from the latter version to the final official wording. See Dvorah Barzilay-Yegar, *A National Home for the Jewish People: The Concept in British Political Thinking and Policy Making, 1917–1923* (Jerusalem: Hassifriaya Haziyonit, 2003), 30 (Hebrew). In view of the above, there will be those who might believe that the wording of important official Zionist documents and public positions does

context is the report which the Jewish Agency for Palestine submitted to the Palestine Royal Commission in 1936 and also to the Anglo-American Committee of Inquiry in 1946. One of the main arguments in the report reads as follows:

> It is asserted that it might similarly be pleaded that the Italians had a claim to a national home in Great Britain because that country had once formed part of the Roman Empire. The conclusive reply to that sophistic argument is that the Italians were never settled in England and that they have, and always have had, a home of their own in Italy, whilst the Jews are not merely the ancient rulers but also the former settlers of Palestine and never had and to this day do not possess any other national home. It is because of that homelessness and because "they have never

---

not provide sufficient evidence to substantiate my claim regarding the moral interpretation of Zionism, namely, that in Zionist ideology, the concept of historical rights refers to rights *in* the Land of Israel rather than rights *over all* of the Land of Israel. Their argument would be that the documents and the public positions in question do not really reflect the "authentic" position of Zionism.

To deal with this objection, a distinction must be drawn between two sorts of cases, namely, those in which the transition from very ambitious goals to more modest ones is a result of acknowledging the constraints imposed by reality and morality on one's ambitious goals, and cases in which this transition is the product of calculated political tactics. Surely, the waiving of ambitious goals and the endorsement of more modest goals, when motivated by one's acknowledgment of pragmatic and moral constraints, does not necessarily indicate that the ambitious goals are the "authentic" ones. The fact is that many of us might have entertained the thought of becoming millionaires or prime ministers but nevertheless gave up these fantasies because we acknowledged the constraints imposed on these ambitions by reality and by our personalities. This does not mean that these ambitions were our authentic ambitions, even though it would not be false to say that we had actually dreamed about such possibilities. However, if we surrender ambitious goals for tactical reasons and express less grandiose goals instead, then it is indeed correct to argue that our first goals are the authentic ones, because the waiver only relates to the immediacy with which the goal is to be achieved or to giving it public expression. It does not mean that we have given up the goal itself.

It is not always possible to determine whether a person's surrender of a particular goal is real or tactical. Even the person herself may be unable to accurately identify her real motivations for giving up a particular goal. For reasons which are beyond the scope of this book, this is especially the case when political leaders abandon goals previously defined for their groups. Briefly, however, this may partly be because members of national groups perceive their nation as existing well beyond their own lifetimes. Thus, what one generation cannot achieve may be thought of as a task for future generations. At any event, even if the surrender of ambitious goals is merely a pretense motivated by tactical considerations, it ought to be remembered that relinquishing ambitious goals in favor of tactical goals may express acknowledgment of the justice of the latter (though this is not always the case). My observation here is somewhat similar to one often made about hypocrites, namely, that their hypocrisy attests to their acknowledgment of the propriety of the standards which they only pretend to follow. Otherwise, they would have no reason for feigning compliance with these particular

forgotten" that the Jews have a claim to the restoration of their national life in Palestine.[11]

The report's admission that the Italians cannot claim sovereignty over Britain necessarily implies recognition that the historical right cannot be the basis for the right to sovereignty as such. However, the quoted passage seems to imply that, in cases of nations lacking a national home, the historical right could be a consideration in determining the geographical site for the realization of their self-determination. According to the passage, by virtue of the fact that they are a homeless nation, the Jews are entitled to reestablish their home *in* Palestine. It does not say that their state of homelessness entitles them to renew their sovereignty over *all of* Palestine. It must also be noted that the Zionist movement has throughout its history been torn by a controversy over whether Jewish self-determination should be realized in all of the Land of Israel or only in part of this territory. From the beginning, and until the establishment of Israel in 1948, controversy raged over whether Jewish self-determination in the Land of Israel should take the form of political sovereignty.[12]

Also, the majority of those who contend that Jewish self-determination should take the form of Jewish political sovereignty have not since argued that this sovereignty must extend over the Land of Israel in its entirety. Again, these facts do not necessarily mean that many Zionists did not consider historical rights as the basis for the right to territorial sovereignty rather than as a basis for selecting the site for self-determination. As already indicated, some of them did in fact think that historical rights justify sovereignty, whereas others were to some degree aware of the fact that historical rights as such could not constitute a basis for demanding territorial sovereignty. However, I am not concerned with the historical question of what actual demands were made by the Zionist

---

standards. In other words, even if one could assume that references by Zionist leaders to a historical right to establish a *national home* for the Jews *within* Palestine rather than a Jewish *state* encompassing Palestine *in its entirety* were tactically rather than strategically motivated, nonetheless, the very adoption of such a tactic seems to express acknowledgment of the fact that these are the morally appropriate terms. It is important to note that the main purpose of this chapter is to deal with what could be interpreted as the aspirations of Zionism in its formative years, and with the question of what Zionism ought to have aspired to based on the historical rights argument, rather than with what any specific Zionist leader aimed for in actual pratice. Even assuming that some of the authors of the Basel Program and the Balfour Declaration did engage in political conniving, and not in the acknowledgment of moral and pragmatic exigencies, the factual questions concerning these people's good faith should not be confused with the actual contents of the Basel Program or the Balfour Declaration.

[11] Quoted in Shimoni, *The Zionist Ideology*, 354.

[12] See chapter 3, notes 1–4, and the argument to which these notes refer.

movement nor with what its leaders and thinkers actually believed when they invoked the historical rights argument. My only concern here is with the moral question of whether a justified version of Zionist ideology is conceivable. In section 2 below, I will claim that invoking historical rights as a consideration for determining the site for the realization of national self-determination, as opposed to relying on such rights in order to demand territorial sovereignty, may be justified or at least excused under certain circumstances and that, in the historical period since the inception of Zionism, there have indeed been times when these circumstances could be said to have existed.

A second important difference between the possible interpretation of the Zionist movement's employment of the historical rights argument and the cases in which other nations have used this argument pertains to the distinction between the primacy of the specific territory in the history of the particular nation and the primacy of the nation in the history of the territory in question. I have already mentioned Otto von Bismarck, who demanded the annexation of Alsace-Lorraine to the German Reich in the wake of the Prussian-French War. In order to justify this claim, he resorted to the fact that these territories had been under German rule in the sixteenth century. Thomas Masaryk's demand to include the Sudetenland in Czechoslovakia after World War I, despite the fact that the Sudetenland was mainly populated by Germans, was backed by a similar claim, namely, that the Sudetenland had been part of the Bohemian kingdom at the end of the Middle Ages. Conceivably, this interpretation of the historical rights argument as a first occupancy argument is also implied in the arguments used by the indigenous peoples of North America, Australia, and New Zealand, most of whom demand that territories usurped by European latecomers be returned to them.[13] Similar demands seem to

---

[13] Regarding the demands of the native nations of the New World against the European settling nations, see David Lyons, "The New Indian Claims and Original Rights to Land," in Jeffrey Paul (ed.), *Reading Nozick: Essays on Anarchy, State and Utopia* (Oxford: Basil Blackwell, 1982), 355–379; Jeremy Waldron, "Superseding Historic Injustice," *Ethics* 103 (1992), 4–28; John A. Simmons, "Historical Rights and Fair Shares," *Law and Philosophy* 14 (1995), 149–184; Margaret Moore, "The Territorial Dimension of Self-Determination," in Margaret Moore (ed.), *National Self-Determination and Secession* (Oxford: Oxford University Press, 1998), 134–157; Andrew Sharp, *Justice and the Māori: The Philosophy and Practice of Māori Claims in New Zealand since the 1970s*, 2nd ed. (Auckland: Oxford University Press, 1997); Ross Poole, *Nation and Identity* (London and New York: Routledge, 1999), chap. 4; Paul Haveman (ed.), *Indigenous Peoples' Rights in Australia, Canada & New Zealand* (Auckland: Oxford University Press, 1999); Duncan Ivison, Paul Patton, and Will Sanders (eds.), *Political Theory and the Rights of Indigenous Peoples* (Cambridge: Cambridge University Press, 2000).

be at play in the dispute between the Tamil and the Sinhalese populations in Sri Lanka.

However, it would seem that when the Zionist movement first invoked the historical rights argument, it focused on the primacy of the Land of Israel in Jewish history and its important role in Jewish identity rather than on the primacy of the Jews in the history of the Land of Israel. In the controversy that broke out at the Sixth Zionist Congress—also known as the Uganda Congress—over what the site for the realization of Jewish self-determination should be, one of the delegates, Franz Oppenheimer, made the following statement: "Allocating [the Jews] the most magnificent expanses of farm land in Canada or Argentina will not enhance the strength of the wandering Jew as much as settling on the lowly Plain through which the Jordan flows and upon which the Lebanon looks out."[14] This quote demonstrates the primacy of the Land of Israel in Jewish identity rather than the primacy of the Jews in the history of the Land of Israel. Clear evidence of the predominance of this conception of the historical right in Zionist annals can be found in Israel's Declaration of Independence. It states, "The Land of Israel was the birthplace of the Jewish people," and it was there that "their spiritual, religious and political identity was shaped," where "they first attained to statehood, created cultural values of national and universal significance." "Impelled by this historic and traditional attachment," the declaration goes on to say, "Jews strove in every successive generation to re-establish themselves in their ancient homeland."[15] Additional formulations of the same idea can be found in the opening declaration of the proposals submitted by the Zionists to the peace conference in Paris in February 1919.[16] They all express a view according to which the experiences which the Jews underwent in Palestine were formative in their becoming a nation and that this is why they were now striving to return to Palestine. As implied in the above documents, the Jews have a historical right to the Land of Israel, not because they were the first among contemporary peoples

---

[14] Quoted in Shmuel Almog, *Zionism and History: The Rise of a New Jewish Consciousness* (New York: St. Martin's, 1987), 259.

[15] *Official Gazette* 1, Tel Aviv, 5 Iyar 5708, 14.5.1948, 1. If one interprets the notion of a nation striving to "re-establish [itself] in [its] ancient homeland" as requiring more than just prayer, then at least the last sentence quoted from Israel's Declaration of Independence is nationalist historiography at its worst. However, see the last paragraph of the introduction to this book and the accompanying notes.

[16] See Shimoni, *The Zionist Ideology*, 352–353.

to occupy it, but rather because it was of primary importance in the formation of their identity.

These differences between the possible interpretations of how early Zionism used the historical rights argument and how other nations have invoked this argument, as well as how it is employed by contemporary Zionism, are of utmost importance. As I will demonstrate below, when historical rights serve as the basis for a claim to sovereignty and territorial expansion, then they lack any validity. They are invalid irrespective of whether they refer to the primacy of a nation in the history of the land, or to the primacy of the land in the history of a nation. However, when the historical rights argument serves as a basis for determining the geographical site for the realization of the right to self-determination, it may under certain circumstances be a sound argument, primarily if it is premised on the interpretation of historical rights as referring to the primacy of the territory in the history and identity of a nation. I will now proceed to elaborate on this point.

2. Historical Rights and Selecting the Site for Self-Determination

The historical rights argument cannot justify the actual right to territorial sovereignty and it cannot serve as a basis for determining the territory's scope. Given the scarcity of resources and space in the world, basing sovereignty rights and their scope on historical rights could endanger the livelihood and autonomy of many peoples. Rousseau stated this point clearly:

> How can a man or a people seize an immense territory and keep it from the rest of the world except by a punishable usurpation, since all other are being robbed, by such an act, of the place of habitation and the means of subsistence which nature gave them in common?[17]

Rousseau's observations were made with regard to first occupants who were physically present in territories over which they claimed sovereignty. However, they are even more applicable to nations which attempt to renew their physical presence in territories where they lived many generations ago. If such nations invoke historical rights to claim territorial sovereignty, then accepting this claim would not only make it impossible for these territories to later be used to satisfy the basic and/or important needs of other people who might need these territories. It would also increase the risk of

[17] Jean-Jacques Rousseau, *The Social Contract* (London: J. M. Dent & Sons, 1920), 20.

uprooting people already living there, and it would necessarily lead to their subordination to foreign rule.

However, if the historical rights argument is regarded not as a basis for the right to territorial sovereignty but rather for the determination of the geographical location in which the nation's right to self-determination is realized, and if self-determination itself is interpreted as less than independent statehood, then the fears expressed above lose a considerable measure of their weight. This is particularly true if considerations of justice serve to determine whether nations are entitled to sovereignty or other territorial rights and what the scope of territories to which these rights apply should be. Based on principles of justice, territories could be allocated to nations according to the size of their respective populations, the nature of their cultures, the specific needs of the cultures, the degree of a nation's commitment to its members, and/or how this nation treats those who are not members. Territory could also be allocated according to a combination of the above criteria as well as additional considerations.[18] Within such a framework, historical rights could serve as a consideration for selecting the specific geographical location where self-determination is to be realized. The area designated for a nation's self-determination may be larger or smaller than the historical territory of that nation. This depends on substantive considerations of distributive justice pertaining to the size of the territories to which each nation is entitled. If the territories of the world are divided between the nations in the world on the basis of these considerations, and if the role of historical rights is interpreted not as a basis for the right to sovereignty but rather as grounds for selecting the location where self-determination is to be realized, then the duties correlative to these rights do not endanger the livelihood and autonomy of many people. People would only have to pay the price of being excluded from specific areas, that is, the areas granted to other nations for the realization of their own right to self-determination. These areas would not be any larger than those from which they would in any case be excluded, provided the territorial rights accompanying self-determination were justly distributed among national groups.

Historical rights should be resorted to for the purpose of selecting the locations of nations' self-determination because there are good reasons

---

[18] Obviously, formulating the principles of justice by which the territories of the world ought to be allocated among the various nations would provoke great controversy. However, it seems reasonable to assume that the considerations listed above would have some import in the process of drafting these principles.

supporting this (and not only because there are no reasons for not doing so). In the case of nations still residing in the territories to which they could claim historical rights, this applies to both conceptions of historical rights, namely, first occupancy and formative territory. If the nation that was the first occupant in a given territory is still in the territory, then first occupancy should be the basis for selecting the site for realizing that nation's right to self-determination. Other grounds for determining this site would require the relocation of entire peoples, and there do not appear to be any good reasons for inflicting such high costs and inconvenience on them. Under the formative territory conception, historical rights should serve as grounds for selecting the location of nations' right to self-determination not only for these pragmatic reasons, but also because it may be very important for people who ascribe great significance to their national affiliation not to be torn away from their national group's formative territory. Being away from their formative territory may arouse feelings of alienation and longing. In view of the importance of formative territories to people's national identities, it can certainly be argued that the link between these territories and the right to national self-determination is an essential one. In contrast to first occupancy, formative territory is not only appropriate grounds for selecting the location of the right to self-determination, but seems to be essential for the realization of this right.[19]

The pragmatic considerations which favor choosing the specific territory in which a given nation was first occupant as the place for realizing its self-determination cease to be valid once the physical connection between the nation and the territory in question has been severed. If over the course of history, a nation ceases to occupy a particular territory, then it can no longer be claimed that its self-determination should be located in that place just because of the need to prevent this particular nation from having to wander from place to place. Quite the opposite is the case. Indeed, any such territorial restitution is likely to force people to wander from place to place. However, the considerations for selecting the site for the realization of self-determination which stem from the formative ties with the homeland do not necessarily lose their force if the physical link between the nation and

---

[19] In support of this view, I will mention that it is subscribed to by authors as remote from one another as Ross Poole, an Australian philosopher who has written about the Aborigines' rights (Poole, *Nation and Identity*, 127–128), and Yechezkel Kaufmann, a Jewish historian who wrote about the Jewish people during the 1930s and 1940s (Yechezkel Kaufmann, *Exile and Foreign Land*, vol. 2 [Tel Aviv: Dvir, 1930], 211–212 [Hebrew]).

the territory has been severed. The interest that the committed members of a nation have in maintaining their link with their formative territory is valid regardless of whether or not they currently occupy the territory. This certainly applies when members of the group have retained an emotional attachment to the place, because it still constitutes a part of their identity. One could claim that the physical separation of the group members from their formative territory is similar to tearing people away from their kin. Such connections usually continue to be a part of people's identities. This constitutes a reason for placing the site of self-determination in the formative territory even when the original physical connection no longer exists.

3. THE PERSECUTION OF THE JEWS

The fact that the nonpragmatic reasons retain their validity for selecting the location of self-determination does not make them conclusive reasons for actually doing so. There are two kinds of considerations that might militate against them. The first kind of consideration pertains to the demographic situation in the territory, the needs of those currently living there, and the needs of those wishing to return to the territory. Consider the case of a Native American tribe whose descendants seek to return to Manhattan in order to resume living there within the framework of their culture. However, due to the large non-Native American population currently living in Manhattan, if members of the tribe were allowed to fulfill their wishes, this would result in the imposition of unreasonably high costs on the other residents of Manhattan. For example, the population density of Manhattan would certainly make it impossible to allow members of the native tribe to live there within the framework of their culture, particularly if it meant that they would have to be provided with hunting grounds. In other words, when a territory is densely populated, this seems to generate other considerations which must override the force of the formative ties as grounds for selecting the site for the realization of the nation's right to self-determination. However, with regard to areas that are not as crowded as New York City and/or cultures that do not require hunting grounds in order to realize their cultural identities, it seems that ethnocultural groups should be entitled to return to these regions provided they have formative ties with these territories.[20] Indeed, in the 1990s, Australian and Canadian

---

[20] The Zionist movement was profoundly aware of this consideration. This is expressed in Israel Zangwill's notorious description of Palestine as a land without a nation, which should

courts recognized the claims of ethnocultural groups to areas with which they have a formative connection in order to realize certain forms of self-determination.[21]

One major difference between the Jews' return to the Land of Israel and the restitution of the title that indigenous groups have to their traditional lands in Australia and Canada is that the latter occurred within the political framework of states that have established legislative and judicial institutions and law enforcement agencies. These institutions draft the principles that define the relationships among all of their subjects, and they settle any disputes which might arise. In contrast, the Jews' return to Palestine occurred in an international context in which such legislative, judicial, and law enforcement institutions were in their embryonic stages.[22] The absence of such institutions in the context of the Jews' return to Palestine forms

---

therefore be given to a nation without a land (Israel Zangvill, "The Return to Palestine," *New Liberal Review* [December 1901], 628). However, those who did not invoke this misleading description stressed the fact that the Land of Israel was not densely populated as one argument in favor of a Jewish return. When justifying the Jewish right over the Land of Israel, Ben-Gurion stated that it arose "from the depopulated state of Eretz Yisrael" (Shimoni, *The Zionist Ideology*, 385).

[21] *Mabo v. Queensland* (no. 2) (1992) 175 CLR 1; *Delgamuukw v. British Columbia* (1997) 153 DLR (4th) 193 (SCC). The links of the Australian aborigines to their lands as the central reason for the change that the *Mabo No. 2* case brought about with regard to their title in their traditional lands is emphasized by Richard H. Bartlett ("Native Title in Australia: Denial, Recognition, and Dispossession," in Haveman (ed.), *Indigenous Peoples' Rights*, pp. 417–418). Other writers (such as Jeremy Webber, "Beyond Regret: *Mabo's* Implications for Australian Constitutionalism," in Ivison, Patton, and Sanders [eds.], *The Rights of Indigenous Peoples*, pp. 72–74) argue that the *Mabo* and *Delgamuukw* decisions pertain not only to property law but also to the constitutional issues of self-determination.

[22] Obviously, there are additional differences, some of which are rather substantial, between the recognition of native nations' title to their traditional lands and the return of the Jews to the Land of Israel. One rather conspicuous difference is that the native groups in the cases referred to in the previous footnote maintained a physical link with their lands, despite the facts that they were denied legal title to these lands and that others also occupied these lands. Another conspicuous difference is that the majority groups currently ruling the New World are the very same groups that denied the native groups title to their lands. They did this hundreds of years ago, so that the ruling majority could be said to be liable for wrongs inflicted on the indigenous groups. Many people would argue that if this kind of liability obtains between the Jews and the Arabs due to the expulsion of the Palestinians and the refugee problem (see my discussion of this issue in chapter 4), then the onus of rectification is on the Jews. There are those who would also make the opposite claim, namely, that the Arabs are the last of a chain of conquerors of the Land of Israel and, as such, their obligation toward the Jewish people is identical to that of the ruling nations in Australia and North America toward the native nations. I will refrain from addressing this theoretical conundrum here.

a second consideration against this return, which must be weighed against the formative tie as a reason for selecting the site of self-determination. It must be noted that formative ties only serve to settle the specific question of location. There is a whole range of additional issues, such as the global distribution of political power and territorial resources among nations, which are relevant to the justice of implementing the right to self-determination. However, in order for justice to be achieved in these matters, there is a need for most nations in the world to coordinate their actions by adhering to a comprehensive system of principles that could help to settle these types of issues. One isolated action according to one principle only that is not part of a comprehensive and institutionalized system could well be compared to playing one single note without completing the performance of the symphony to which it belongs. However, in the case of justice, in contrast to the analogy of music, playing an isolated note is not merely jarring. Applying one isolated principle of justice to only one party may mean that this party alone might be forced to pay a price which ought to have been shared by all those subject to the aforementioned system of principles.[23] As illustrated below, this isolated action may also confer advantages to parties who may not be the only ones entitled to those advantages.

In this context, there is another related issue that also warrants consideration. If the burdens and advantages of distributive justice are not allocated among all of the parties involved (in our case, the nations of the world), and if only one of them pays the price (perhaps rightfully so, but others should also have to pay the price), and if only one of them reaps the benefits (again, perhaps rightfully so, but others should also reap the benefits), then it is reasonable to expect that this might lead to instability and possibly even bloodshed.[24] In other words, even if the formative tie which a particular nation has to a given territory should ideally be a reason to make that territory the site for the realization of the nation's self-determination

---

[23] For example, if it is deemed appropriate for the Palestinians to allow the Jews to select the site of their self-determination in Palestine, then they should be given territory in compensation for the territories they have lost or at least be compensated financially by the other nations of the world.

[24] Regarding the degree to which the different streams of Zionism were aware of the possibility of bloodshed as a result of the implementation of the Zionist goals, the different interpretations of the sources of this danger, and what might have prevented it, see Anita Shapira, *Land and Power: The Zionist Resort to Force, 1881–1948*, trans. William Templer (New York: Oxford University Press, 1992); and Yosef Gorny, *Zionism and the Arabs, 1882–1948: A Study of Ideology*, trans. Chaya Galai (Oxford: Clarendon, 1987).

(provided the geodemographic conditions of that territory allow this), in our non-ideal world, considerations both of justice (the equal distribution of burdens and benefits to all parties involved) and of morality (prevention of bloodshed) compel the suspension of any action according to this ideal.[25] To illustrate this point, consider those who believe that Saudi Arabia should not be the only country to profit from the oil on its territory and that it should share oil revenues with countries suffering from abject poverty, such as Somalia. A person subscribing to this position need not necessarily think that this principled stand entails the conclusion that Somalia has the right to invade Saudi Arabia and appropriate its portion of the oil wealth in question. It could be contended that Saudi Arabia should not be the only one to have to share its oil with other countries. Kuwait should also do so, and not only Somalia but also Chad, for instance, should benefit from this. It might even be contended that the reallocation of wealth should not be limited to revenues generated from natural resources owned by nations, but should also include wealth derived from human talent and investments. Furthermore, these allocation issues should be regulated by a public system consisting of principles that are acceptable to most or all of its subjects and enforced by judicial and executive authorities capable of applying these principles in a coordinated and consistent manner. Consequently, any isolated and unilateral action against one of the parties subject to these principles would be at least partially unjust and might lead to bloodshed, even if the justice of the principle itself is undisputed.

Under normal circumstances, this last argument should convince members of nations to refrain from returning to their historical homelands. However, in the absence of real alternatives for realizing their self-determination,

---

[25] This distinction resembles the distinction made by John Rawls, *A Theory of Justice* (Cambridge, MA: Harvard University Press, 1971), between ideal and non-ideal theories of justice. An ideal theory establishes the principles to which society should aspire and which it should endorse, under the assumption of full compliance with these principles. A similar distinction is made by rule utilitarians between the desirable set of rules in a situation of full compliance and the desirable set of rules in a situation of partial compliance. On the use of this distinction in the context of international law and justice, see Allen Buchanan, *Justice, Legitimacy, and Self-Determination: Moral Foundations for International Law* (New York: Oxford University Press, 2004). As mentioned in the chapter, the view that high population density in a given territory precludes invoking formative ties even as a consideration for selecting the site of self-determination is valid even within an ideal theory of distributive justice. On the other hand, the argument that the absence of publicly recognized authorities for drafting these principles and enforcing them precludes invoking the formative ties as a consideration for selecting the site of self-determination is only valid in the context of a non-ideal theory of distributive justice.

or at least a lack of a feasible way to lead reasonable lives as individuals, it would not be unreasonable for members of a national group to nevertheless resort to the historical rights argument. It could be argued that necessity could justify resorting to the historical rights argument in such circumstances or, at least, constitutes a good excuse from liability for those who resort to and act on it. In hindsight, the situation in Europe at the end of the nineteenth century was one in which the Jews had only the very dimmest chances to realize their self-determination there, as envisioned by the Bund, or even to continue living as individuals in a manner that would ensure their survival. On the other hand, the realization of Jewish self-determination in eastern Africa, as advocated by the territorialists at the beginning of the twentieth century, suffered from the same deficiencies that affected the Zionist call to realize Jewish self-determination in the Land of Israel, but without its attendant benefits. Like the realization of Jewish self-determination in the Land of Israel, Jewish self-determination in eastern Africa was to be realized in territory that had long been the home of another ethnocultural group. Settling this territory could well lead to brutal conflict with them. On the other hand, the realization of Jewish self-determination in East Africa, as opposed to its realization in the Land of Israel, could not be based on formative historical ties. Many Jews had been victims of persecution and could not continue living where they were currently living both as individuals and as a group. Under these conditions, it seems that these Jews could not reasonably be expected to act on the principle that many actions required by ideal justice had to be suspended because of the partial injustice and even bloodshed to which such actions might lead.

The necessity which, according to the current account, supports resorting to the historical rights argument is very similar to the "necessity" defense in criminal law. This defense is often invoked to justify acts that would be legally and morally prohibited under normal circumstances, or at least to excuse those committing these acts from liability. Although I believe that the persecution of the Jews constituted a necessity that justified the return to Palestine, it is not an incontrovertible case of a justifying necessity. There might well be those who would regard the persecution of the Jews as merely excusing them from liability.[26] An example in which necessity incontrovertibly

---

[26] Regarding the distinction between necessity that fully justifies a criminal action, and necessity that excuses from culpability without justifying the action, and for a generally illuminating and captivating discussion of the necessity defense, see George Fletcher, *Rethinking Criminal Law* (Boston: Little, Brown, 1978), chap. 10.

justifies an act that otherwise would be considered criminal and immoral
is that of the mortally wounded person who has no way of saving her life
other than by breaking into a pharmacy to steal the required medicine. On
the other hand, a necessity which cannot justify the act itself but nevertheless could be invoked as an excuse from liability is illustrated by the ancient
example of two men shipwrecked at sea: One of the two manages to grab
hold of a plank, from which he is then pushed off by the other man. The
evil caused by the criminal act in the pharmacy example is an infinitely lesser
evil than the evil that would have been caused if the crime had not been
committed. Therefore, the necessity involved is incontrovertibly a justifying
necessity. In the plank example, on the other hand, the two evils (the death
of either of the two people) are of the same magnitude. It could at most serve
as an excuse against liability.[27] The pharmacy analogy is intended to convey
the idea that Palestine could offer the Jews medication, as it were, for healing
the malady of having been persecuted and of being helpless in confront-
ing this persecution. However, this medication was not of the kind that was
on the pharmacy shelf ready to be collected by a person who then leaves the
pharmacy. Rather, the medication consisted in taking permanent possession
of part of the pharmacy itself. It is therefore not as incontrovertible a case
of justifying necessity as that of the mortally wounded person breaking into
the pharmacy. On the other hand, it does not seem to be as clear-cut a case
of an excuse from liability as that of the plank. In the latter case, in order to
save himself, one drowning man must drown the other.[28]

---

[27] There are two reasons for excusing perpetrators from liability in cases such as the
drowning example. One emanates from the law's inability to deter people from committing
the crime because the legal punishment awaiting the wrongdoer is less threatening than what
she could expect if she did not commit the crime in question. (See Thomas Hobbes, *Leviathan*
[Oxford: A. R. Mowbray & Co., 1946], 196–197; Immanuel Kant, *The Metaphysical Elements of
Justice*, trans. John Ladd [Indianapolis: Bobbs-Merrill, 1965], 41.) Another possible reason for
excusing perpetrators from liability in cases such as the drowning example is their weakened
capacity for rational judgment and action in such situations.

[28] Other doubts concerning the applicability of the defense of necessity to the case of
the Jewish return to Palestine could emerge from two further conditions which must obtain
for the defense to apply. One condition is that the perpetrator of the criminal act must be in
imminent and certain danger. Another condition is that this particular criminal act must be
the only means available for the prevention of the danger. It could be argued that with the rise
of anti-Semitism and Nazism in the 1930s, especially when the death camps began operating
in 1942, these conditions were satisfied in a far more conclusive manner than at the end of
the nineteenth century and the beginning of the twentieth century. However, there are cases
in which courts have applied the necessity defense and acquitted perpetrators of criminal acts
even when the perpetrator was not in imminent danger and even when the act committed

But let me return to the historical rights argument. It provides a response to the query that some Arabs might come up with: "Why our pharmacy?" The response is either "Because it is the only one carrying the appropriate medicine" or "Because the medicine carried here is better than the medicines found in other pharmacies" (that is, places such as Uganda, Eastern Europe, or Argentina). The medicine, as it were, is a unique one, or is in any case better than any other available solution to the problem. That is, an attempt to realize self-determination in the formative territory has a chance of succeeding, or at least has better chances of success than any attempts to realize self-determination in other territories might have. In the above account, the role of the necessity defense in general and the analogy of the pharmacy in particular is to emphasize what should have been emphasized from the very beginning, namely, that the reasons militating against the realization of Jewish self-determination in Palestine—stemming from the injustice that this would create and from the expected bloodshed—were overridden by or ignored because of the Jews' urgent need,

---

was not clearly the only way to avoid danger or even the most reasonable method for protecting the perpetrator from danger. Fletcher records two such cases. In one of them, a son was acquitted of killing his father. When the son killed his father, neither he nor the family was in imminent danger. However, there had been a protracted history of domestic violence; the father had been terrorizing the other members of the family. In another case, a person burned down a house that he had received from the local housing authority. He claimed that the house was about to collapse and constituted a severe safety hazard endangering the lives of its inhabitants. He claimed that the only way to galvanize the local housing authority into providing alternative housing for his family was to burn down the house (Fletcher, *Rethinking Criminal Law*, 820).

The Jews had been persecuted for hundreds of years. The Enlightenment, the Emancipation of the Jews in Europe during the eighteenth and nineteenth centuries, and their willingness to assimilate into the nations among which they were living did not alleviate their plight. At any rate, many of them had good reasons for feeling that their situation had not improved. It might be argued that the conjunction of the history of persecution and the fact that the Enlightenment did not eradicate persecution allows a certain analogy to be drawn between the situation faced by the Jews at the end of the nineteenth century and the beginning of the twentieth century and that of the person who killed his father after suffering from a long history of severe domestic violence. In both cases, feelings of despair that result from a history of persecution and terror exempt the perpetrators of the crime from culpability for actions that are not really justified. The situation in which the Jews found themselves in at the turn of the twentieth century (and perhaps even up to the 1930s and 1940s) could perhaps also be considered analogous to the case of the house on the verge of collapse: Even if it cannot be incontrovertibly asserted that the means that the Jews employed to extricate themselves from their plight (their return to an already settled land to realize their self-determination) was the only or the most reasonable means of protecting themselves against the anticipated danger, they should be exempt from liability for employing such means.

both as individuals and as a people, to ensure their physical safety and to retain their dignity by realizing their right to self-determination and not by the Jews' right to self-determination itself and the ordinary reasons supporting this right (people's interest in living within the framework of their cultures and determining their destinies within their culture).[29]

According to the above analysis, the Zionist principle calling for a return to the Land of Israel is complex. It views the historical right not as a basis for rights to territorial sovereignty, but rather as grounds for selecting the geographical site for realizing the right to self-determination. This right is not necessarily a right to statist sovereignty. Such sovereignty is

---

[29] The combination of the right to self-determination and the necessity which justified the urgent implementation of this right in the case of the Jews is one that also figures prominently in traditional Zionist justifications for the Jews' return to Palestine. I am referring to justifications such as those espoused by statesmen like Jabotinsky (see Shimoni, *The Zionist Ideology*, 366–369) and Ben-Gurion (ibid., 385), and writers such as Gafni (ibid., 356). Furthermore, it would appear that none of them regarded these arguments or any other argument (such as the historical rights argument or the argument that Palestine was sparsely populated at the inception of Zionism) as independently sufficient to justify the Jews' return. They seem to have felt that each of these arguments or a combination of them was necessary in order to justify the return of the Jews, but that only the combination of all of the arguments was sufficient for this purpose. However, they do not seem to be aware of the specific role that each of these arguments plays in this justification. At least, they are not explicit on this point. Likewise, they do not seem to acknowledge the fact that even the combination of all of these arguments only justifies the realization of *self-determination in* Palestine and not *sovereignty over* the whole of Palestine. However, Jabotinsky's comments indicate that he seemed to be somewhat aware of at least some of these matters. On one occasion, he stated that "[the] first question is 'have you a need for land?' If you have no need, if you have sufficient, then you may not rest your case on historical rights" (Shimoni, *The Zionist Ideology*, 367). On the other hand, in his testimony before the Peel Committee in 1937, he justified his demand to establish a state on both banks of the Jordan not by resorting to historical rights, but rather by invoking the amount of territory he deemed necessary for settlements that would be the home of four million Jews. See Itzhak Galnoor, *Territorial Partition: Decision Crossroads in the Zionist Movement* (Jerusalem: Magnes, 1994), 87–88, 170 (Hebrew). See also the testimonial lecture by Benjamin Aktzin concerning the revisionist Zionists' position on the partition plan, published in Meir Avizohar and Isaiah Friedman (eds.), *Studies in the Palestine Partition Plans, 1937–1947* (Sede Boqer: Ben-Gurion Research Center, 1984), 160–165 (Hebrew). It could perhaps be argued that Jabotinsky's comments show that he was aware of the distinctions among justifying the right to self-determination, justifying the territorial scope of this right, and justifying its geographical site, and that he was cognizant of the fact that each of these issues requires an answer based on different categories of considerations. Jabotinsky commented that "[the] first question is 'have you a need for land?' " Otherwise, he believed, one cannot invoke historical rights. Perhaps this also indicates that he seemed to distinguish between resorting to the historical rights argument within an ideal theory of global justice and resorting to this argument in our non-ideal world, where only urgent needs can justify the invocation of the argument.

just one possible interpretation or possible manifestation of the right to self-determination. There are many other possible and more modest manifestations of this right. In addition, it must also be stressed that invoking historical rights as grounds for selecting the location for the realization of the right to self-determination does not mean that this self-determination must necessarily extend over the whole area with which the nation in question has historical ties. As indicated above, the right to select the site of national self-determination in a historical territory even if the nation in question stopped living in the territory sometime in the past is a primary one, rather than a remedial one.[30] However, it forms a part of an ideal theory of global distributive justice among nations. Because our non-ideal world does not have institutions for formulating the specifics of the principles of this theory in a way that would facilitate their enforcement and also does not have institutions for enforcing such principles, there are good reasons for suspending the right to realize self-determination in a historic homeland. Specifically, injustice and almost certain bloodshed would ensue if this right were realized in such circumstances. Nonetheless, in cases in which people are persecuted to the degree experienced by European Jewry, they have a remedial justification for exercising this right or, at least, must be excused for exercising it.

This analysis of the Zionist principle calling for the Jews' return to the Land of Israel could shed light on some of the underlying conceptual and moral sources of many of the disputes between Zionism and its rivals and within the Zionist movement itself at various stages of its history. For example, the distinction between historical rights as grounds for selecting the site for national self-determination and, on the other hand, historical rights as grounds for the actual right to sovereignty could explain the conceptual origins of the disputes that have divided Zionism since its inception regarding the desirable institutional and territorial dimensions of Jewish

---

[30] A *remedial justification* or *remedial right* is a justification or right that people have by virtue of a harm caused to fundamental interests they have and/or harm caused to interests they have which are protected by primary rights. A remedial right is conferred in order to halt or remedy such harm. A *primary right* is a right that people have by virtue of interests they have in the normal course of their lives (excluding interests they have in emergency situations); primary rights justify the imposition of duties on others in order to protect those interests. Primary rights may be granted in order to protect or promote these interests even in cases in which they are not already being harmed. For example, a person's right not to be attacked is a primary right. Rights or justifications that we have to perform certain acts in order to rescue ourselves from attacks or rights to compensation for harm caused by attacks are remedial rights or justifications.

self-determination in Palestine. Examples of such disputes were those between early leaders and the founders of Zionism, such as Ahad Ha'am and Herzl, between the socialist movement of Hashomer Hatzair and the right-wing revisionist faction within Zionism in the decades before the establishment of the State of Israel, and between Israeli left- and right-wing political parties today. They all seem to share one core idea, namely, that Jewish self-determination should indeed be realized in Palestine. However, they have been divided on the issue of the appropriate institutional form of Jewish self-determination and the size of the territory considered to be appropriate for this purpose.

The distinction between the role that formative ties can play within an ideal system of justice and the inappropriateness of allowing them to play this role in our non-ideal world may shed some light on the moral origins of the dispute between the approaches called political Zionism and practical Zionism. *Political Zionism* strove to secure support for a Jewish national home from a great power or an international organization and held that the Jewish national home must be guaranteed by international law. According to *practical Zionism*, on the other hand, the goals of Zionism would be achieved by establishing Jewish settlements in Palestine and creating facts on the ground. It may be reasonable to presume that the dispute between these two general approaches to Zionism was primarily motivated by pragmatic considerations. However, it may still be argued that political Zionism was more open to the fact that the historical rights argument could only serve as grounds for selecting the site for the realization of self-determination in the framework of an ideal theory of global justice. It could be said that the rationale behind political Zionism was to overcome the deficiencies of our non-ideal world, which lacks authorized institutions for applying the principles of global justice, by seeking the support of great powers and international institutions that would perhaps be able to rule on disputes and attempt to minimize the bloodshed likely to occur as a result of such international conflicts.

The political struggle between the Bund and the Zionist parties in eastern Europe in the first few decades of the twentieth century reflects another issue mentioned above, namely, the distinction among the role of historical rights within ideal global justice, the need to suspend action according to such rights in our non-ideal world, and the justification which persecution could provide for lifting this suspension. As noted above, the Bund strove to achieve self-determination for the Jews in eastern Europe, while Zionism aspired to achieve this goal in Palestine. These two parties received more or less equal support from the Jewish public in eastern Europe in the first few decades of the twentieth century. This equal political support by the Jewish public can be explained by the fact that it was not until the 1930s that the persecution of the Jews became serious enough to create an incontrovertible necessity for the Jews to realize their right to self-determination in Palestine. Although the pogroms which took place in southern Russia in the 1880s were sufficiently tumultuous to have given rise to the eastern European movement of Hibbat Zion, a forerunner of Zionism,[31] and the Dreyfus affair was powerful enough to have turned Herzl into a Zionist, neither of these was sufficiently powerful to outweigh concerns about the impending injustice to the Arabs living in Palestine and about any possible conflict.

If it had not been for the Nazi rise to power and the Holocaust, Zionism might not have emerged triumphant, and the Bund might not have withered into insignificance. The inherent complexity of the Zionist principle calling for the return of the Jews to the Land of Israel could help to explain this commonly held and probably correct view. It is the Nazi rise to power and the Holocaust that followed which ultimately rendered the persecution of Jews shocking to the extent that it demanded an urgent solution. Although the recourse to historical rights as a consideration for selecting the site for the realization of the right to self-determination must be suspended in our non-ideal world, it is reasonable to claim that the rationale for this suspension could be overridden by this unique situation.

4. RESPONDING TO ARAB OPPOSITION TO ZIONISM

The above analysis of the Zionist principle concerning the Jews' return to Palestine also implies an important explanation for the Arabs' opposition to the Jews' return. It is quite certain that this opposition was due to the instinctive unwillingness of most individuals and groups of individuals to share something they possess with others (especially if these other people are strangers), even when justice mandates redistribution. However, even if Arab opposition were motivated by this instinct, it was also motivated by justified objections to Zionism. Some of these objections are valid because,

---

[31] In Hebrew, the expression *Hibbat Zion* literally means "fondness of Zion." The eastern European groups belonging to this movement were the forerunners of the Zionist movement. They were established in the early 1880s in order to promote Jewish immigration to the Land of Israel.

as I will argue later in this book, in various periods, the Zionist movement actually seized far more than was justified in terms of both political power and territory. However, the Arabs' objection to the Zionist return was partly justified even with respect to those components of Zionist ideology and activities which are unequivocally justified. As implied by the theoretical distinction outlined earlier, the Arabs could claim as follows:

> According to an ideal theory of global justice, it could be the case that the Jews were indeed justified in selecting the site of their self-determination in Palestine. However, there was no institution which could effectively determine the size of the territory and the political scope of Jewish self-determination, and there certainly were no law enforcement institutions to make the world's nations share the cost of all this. The fact that the Jews selected the site for the realization of their self-determination in territory currently inhabited by us, even if they might have been entitled to do so, ultimately exacted a price only from us, whereas all of the nations of the world should have shared this cost. Therefore, even if it might have been justified for the Jews to return to Palestine in the best of possible worlds, the actual state of the world meant that it was also justified for us to object to their return.

The Arabs could also claim the following: "The Jews returned to Palestine due to a necessity that arose as a result of their persecution by the European nations and not by us, but this occurred without a system that would ensure that the Jews and/or these nations compensate us for the injustice inflicted on us by that return."

Consider again the example of the pharmacy cited above. Many systems of justice grant the defense of necessity to people who find themselves in life-threatening situations and who are able to rescue themselves only by committing acts which would otherwise be considered criminal offenses, such as breaking into a store and stealing life-saving drugs. They recognize this defense either as a justification of the act or at least as an excuse from liability. However, domestic systems of law and justice are also in a position to enact and enforce additional principles which lessen or even eliminate the cost that store owners are forced to incur as a result of the recognition of the necessity defense in such cases. They could determine that, if the burglar's injury were caused by other parties, then the burglar and those other parties should indemnify the pharmacy owner; or, they could determine that, if the burglar's injury were a result of natural forces or an accident for which no one in particular was responsible, then the burglar and the public at large should indemnify the pharmacy owner. As I noted earlier, in the global context in which the Jews exercised their right to self-determination, there were no acknowledged principles sufficiently detailed to settle such matters; there was no institution authorized to formulate them at a degree of specificity that would facilitate their enforcement; and there was no authority or organization which could enforce them. In other words, even if one concedes that the Jews had a justification for the realization of their self-determination in Palestine at a time when they were being persecuted by the European nations, one must admit that the Arabs living in Palestine also had significant justifications for refusing to let them do so.[32] One must concede that this case is different from that of a pharmacy owner who would have no justification for refusing to supply a mortally wounded person with a specific kind of medicine that could only be found in his store. Not only did the Jews break into the Arabs' pharmacy as it were in order to settle there rather than merely take a specific medication and then leave, the Arabs had no assurance regarding the upper limit of their potential losses and any compensation for such losses. I do not claim that the Arabs' justifications for resisting the Jewish return to Palestine were necessarily conclusive, but they were certainly cogent.[33]

[32] Following German jurisprudence, Fletcher holds the view that in cases of justifying necessity, resistance to the perpetrator cannot be justified. It is only in cases in which the necessity merely excuses the perpetrator from liability that resistance could be justified. However, some scholars object to this view. See Joshua Dressler, *New Thoughts about the Concept of Justification in the Criminal Law: A Critique of Fletcher's Thinking and Rethinking*, UCLA Law Review 32 (1984), 61–69 at 89–91.

[33] It is common among Israeli speakers to blame the Arabs for their own suffering because of their stubbornness in consistently refusing to accept partition plans for Palestine, mainly the United Nations General Assembly 1947 partition plan. According to the analysis suggested here, it could be said that their resistance to Zionism in 1947 was the least justified in comparison to any other points in time during the Jewish-Arab conflict. However, their resistance cannot be said to have been entirely unjustified. On the one hand, in 1947, just two years after the end of World War II and the Holocaust, the Jews' justifications for establishing their self-determination in Palestine were stronger than ever. On the other hand, the UN Assembly's Partition Resolution could be considered as an authoritative international solution for the problem of the price that the Arabs would have to pay for the Jewish return to Palestine. The absence of an authoritative determination of this price was one of the reasons why the Arabs' resistance to the Jewish return was justified. Nevertheless, it could be said that the Arabs' resistance was still justified after the 1947 UN Partition Resolution. This resolution only required the Arabs to pay a price for the Jewish return to Palestine. Yet according to the justification for this return outlined in this chapter, and as explicated below, this price should have been shared by all the world nations, and especially the European nations. Moreover, it could also be argued that the UN resolution provided further justification for the Arabs' resistance. It was clear at the time that they were bound to be the only ones to pay the price for the Jewish return not only because of the Jewish return itself but also in view of the authority that a resolution by an international body had. Surely they could not accept this.

In view of the above, Jews have a special moral obligation to understand Arab opposition to their return to the Land of Israel and to try to contain it by way of conciliation. However, the complex justification presented here for the Zionist principle calling for the Jews' return to Palestine could explain another prevailing insight pertaining to the Jewish-Arab dispute over Palestine, namely, the notion that all of the nations in the world, particularly the European nations, and especially Germany, are responsible for this conflict.[34] The nations of the world are responsible for the conflict because the main component of the justification for the Jews' return to the Land of Israel is a principle pertaining to global distributive justice, according to which each nation should be entitled to a political and territorial portion of its historical homeland. As noted above, the implementation of this principle in the case of the Jews led to a situation where only the Arabs paid the required price.

However, the principle in question is part of a general system of justice that applies to all nations. All nations, or at least those capable of doing so, should therefore be obliged to incur the cost of the realization of this system. They are morally obliged to assist in the conciliation of the Arabs and then in compensating them for the price that they have paid. For example, in the context of peace negotiations with the Palestinian Authority, former Israeli prime minister Ehud Barak suggested that Canada and Australia admit Palestinian refugees.[35] Such an act could be justified in terms of the above duty. The special liability of the European nations, primarily Germany, to appease and conciliate the Palestinians and to assist the Israelis in compensating them could be explained by the role played by these nations in creating the necessity for the Jews to return to Palestine. The Russian pogroms and the Dreyfus affair in France brought about the awakening of Zionism, and the nations responsible for these and similar events have a special responsibility to conciliate and compensate the Arabs. This goes beyond the responsibility deriving from global distributive justice, which they share with all other nations. And since the German persecution of the Jews created a situation which rendered Zionism more just than it had been in any previous situation, the Germans have a greater responsibility for compensating the Arabs and for assisting Israel than any other nation. Indeed, since the 1960s, many people in Germany have subscribed to this position.

---

[34] I assume here that it is indeed possible to attribute responsibility to national groups.

[35] See Uria Shavit and Jalal Bana, "The Palestinian Dream, the Israeli Nightmare," Ha'aretz (July 6, 2001) (Hebrew).

I hope to have demonstrated that the Zionist movement's aspiration to establish self-determination for the Jews in the Land of Israel had significant justifications. Yet, the precise institutional form of this self-determination, that is, whether or not it should be in the form of a state, and what should be the size of the territory in which this self-determination is realized are questions which the discussion thus far has not addressed. I will discuss these issues in the following chapters. The question of the appropriate institutional form of self-determination for the Jewish people in the Land of Israel will be discussed in chapters 3 and 5. The issue of the territorial dimension of this self-determination will be dealt with in chapter 4.

3

A Jewish State

Self-Determination and Hegemony

The upshot of the previous chapters is that Zionism cannot be rejected merely because it is a nationalist ideology of the ethnocultural type, nor because its ideology supports the principle of the return of the Jewish people to Palestine in order to realize their right to self-determination. The assertion of the right to self-determination is one of the central tenets of ethnocultural nationalism. According to this type of nationalism, people's interest in adhering to their culture and in sustaining it for generations should be politically protected by means of the right to self-determination and self-rule. However, this right can be realized in a variety of institutional forms. That is, self-rule and self-determination could be substatist and nonterritorial, substatist and territorial, or it could take the form of a nation-state in which the ethnocultural group enjoys hegemony (or even exclusivity).

At least until the 1930s, the desire to realize the Jewish right to self-determination in a hegemonic and statist form in Palestine was not prevalent among Zionist activists and thinkers. This at least reflected Zionist aspirations as expressed by Zionist institutions and the supportive proclamations issued by the great powers and international bodies. Admittedly, Herzl dreamed of a Jewish state, but the Basel Program, which he presented at the First Zionist Congress in 1898, defined Zionism as aiming for the "establishment of a home for the Jewish people secured under public law in Palestine."[1] At the beginning of the twentieth century, Ahad Ha'am spoke of the creation of a "spiritual center" in the Land of Israel.[2] In 1917, Chaim Weizmann, a leading Zionist statesman who was later elected the first

---

[1] Quoted in Ben Halpern, *The Idea of the Jewish State*, 2nd ed. (Cambridge, MA: Harvard University Press, 1969), 28.

[2] On Ahad Ha'am's notion of a spiritual center, see Steven J. Zipperstein, *Elusive Prophet: Ahad Ha'am and the Origins of Zionism* (Los Angeles: University of California Press, 1993), chap. 3.

president of the State of Israel, succeeded in convincing the British foreign minister to issue what later became known as the Balfour Declaration regarding the establishment of a "national home" for the Jews in Palestine.[3] At the beginning of the 1920s, even Ze'ev Jabotinsky, the founder of the right-wing Revisionist faction within Zionism, still spoke in terms of a binational "Jewish-Arab federation." In 1931, he proposed that the Zionist Congress declare the establishment of a state in the Land of Israel as the final goal of Zionism, but his proposal was rejected.[4] It was only in the 1930s with the rise of fascism in Germany, anti-Semitism in Poland, and the

[3] See chapter 2, note 9.

[4] Regarding the fact that Zionist ambitions for the institutional form of Jewish self-determination in the Land of Israel were modest, see Halpern, *The Idea of the Jewish State*, 21–23. Halpern examines this aspect of Zionist history from the Basel Program of the First Zionist Congress in 1897 until the negotiations with the United Nations' mission regarding the implementation of the General Assembly's partition plan of November 29, 1947. Halpern contends that this modesty is one of the hallmarks of the Zionist movement, which distinguishes it from other national movements. However, it is not entirely correct to view modesty in this respect as a phenomenon unique to Zionism. See my discussion in Chaim Gans, *The Limits of Nationalism* (Cambridge: Cambridge University Press, 2003), 23–26. The modesty of Zionist aspirations regarding the institutional form of Jewish self-determination in the Land of Israel is emphasized in most of the historical accounts I referred to in chapter 2, and presumably in many other sources. See also Yosef Gorny's book *Policy and Imagination: Federal Ideas in Zionist Political Thought, 1917–1948* (Jerusalem: Yad Izhak Ben-Zvi, Hassifriya Haziyonit, 1993) (Hebrew), which deals with the plans for something less than a state in the political ideas expressed by Jabotinsky, Ben-Gurion, Weizmann, and others; and Itzhak Galnoor, *Territorial Partition: Decision Crossroads in the Zionist Movement* (Jerusalem: Magnes, 1994) (Hebrew).

Of course, it could be argued that this modesty was the product of diplomatic pressure and pragmatic and moral constraints and that, despite what documents such as the Basel Program and the Balfour Declaration reveal, what the Zionist movement and its leaders "really" aspired to was to establish a state in which the Jewish people would enjoy hegemony in the Land of Israel in its entirety. In note 10 in chapter 2, in addressing the desirable interpretation of the historical rights argument in order to come up with a just interpretation of Zionist ideology, I discussed a similar claim regarding the territorial aspirations of Zionism. The claim was that the Zionist talk of establishing a Jewish political entity in the Land of Israel served to conceal an attempt to establish a Jewish state in the whole country. The relationship between entertaining very ambitious goals and withdrawing from such goals, which I discussed there, also applies here. In this context, I note that it is mainly a group of historians known as the "New Historians" who claim that the real goals of Zionism were much more ambitious than those expressed in the official decisions of Zionist institutions and by some Zionist leaders. They claim that the apparent modesty of many of the official decisions and statements made by Zionist leaders should be attributed to mere tactical considerations. See Benny Morris, "The New Historiography: Israel Confronts Its Past," *Tikkun* 3(6) (1988), 19–23, 99–102; Avi Shlaim, *Collusion across the Jordan: King Abdullah, the Zionist Movement, and the Partition of Palestine* (New York: Columbia University Press, 1988); Ilan Pappé, *Britain and the Arab-Israeli Conflict 1948–51* (New York: St. Martin's, 1988).

Arab rebellion in Palestine (1936–1939) that establishing a state became a peremptory Zionist demand. It became the defining ideal of Zionism during and after the Second World War.[5]

In present-day Israel, the principle of Jewish hegemony in the State of Israel is sacrosanct. It enjoys constitutional status in Israel's basic laws and rules in many other important areas as well: citizenship and immigration, land acquisition, education, political participation, employment and resource allocation, legal interpretation, state symbols, the state's name and anthem, names of places, titles of institutions, language, and official holidays. This chapter deals with the hegemonic aspect of contemporary Zionism.

In Israeli public discourse, four arguments are usually invoked in order to justify the principle of Jewish hegemony. The first argument concerns the identification of the right to national self-determination with a right to a nation-state. In the public discourse among Jewish Israelis,[6] it is virtually presupposed that self-determination means the right to sovereignty or the hegemony of one ethnocultural group in a state of its own.[7] The second argument frequently invoked by Israeli Jews to justify the hegemonic interpretation of the Jewish right to self-determination in Israel is that most or at least many states view themselves in this manner.[8] A third argument appeals to the long

[5] The important institutional manifestation of this position was the Biltmore Program of 1942 (adopted as a resolution by a conference of various Zionist and non-Zionist Jewish organizations that was held in the Biltmore Hotel in New York City). Nonetheless, even during the decisive months between the partition plan passed by the United Nations on November 29, 1947, and the Declaration of Independence with which the State of Israel was formally established on May 14, 1948, the Jews were ready to accept limitations on the scope of that hegemony. See Halpern, *The Idea of the Jewish State*, 370–378.

[6] Israel's population consists of a Jewish majority and an Arab minority, the members of which are also Israeli citizens (versus Arabs living in the occupied territories, who are not citizens of Israel).

[7] See, for example, the opinion expressed by Justice Dov Levine in EA 2/88, *Ben Shalom v. The Central Elections Committee for the Twelfth Knesset*, P.D. 43(4), 221 (Hebrew). In her defense of Israel as a Jewish nation-state, Ruth Gavison, a reputable law professor at the Hebrew University and a prominent public figure, uses the following definition: "A nation state—a state whose institutions and official public culture are linked to a particular national group—offers special benefits to the people with whom the state is identified. At the same time, it puts those citizens who are not members of the preferred national community at a disadvantage." Ruth Gavison, "The Jews' Right to Statehood: A Defense," *Azure* 15 (2003), 74–75.

[8] Alexander Yakobson and Amnon Rubinstein repeat this argument many times in their book *Israel and the Family of Nations: Jewish Nation-State and Human Rights* (Tel Aviv: Schocken, 2003) (Hebrew). Utilizing numerous examples from other states, the book attempts to prove that Israel is not exceptional in its self-perception as a hegemonic nation-state. In this context, I will also mention the comments of a former president of the Israeli Supreme Court, Meir

history of persecution suffered by Jews, which occurred largely with the support of the governments of the states in which they lived.[9] Finally, these three arguments are supplemented by a fourth one that relies on the long and bloody conflict between Jews and Arabs in Palestine/Israel.

In the first section of this chapter, I will explain why the right which ethnocultural groups have to self-determination should not be interpreted as the right of such groups to hegemony in the countries in which they exercise self-determination. Rather, it should be understood under a far more modest conception. In the second section of the chapter, I will argue that the hegemonic interpretation of Jewish self-determination neverthe-less became justified in the wake of the Nazi ascent to power and the Arab revolt. This is mainly due to the history of Jewish persecution and the Jew-ish-Arab conflict, respectively, and, to a lesser extent, because of the hege-monic practices of many nation-states. However, I will claim that even if these three arguments do justify the implementation of the hegemonic conception in Israel, they are of limited force both in terms of the kind of justification that they provide and in terms of their substantive scope. That is, they are circumstantial rather than principled, and they only apply to the domains of demography (by which I mean the numerical balance between the Jewish and Arab populations) and security. Moreover, though some of the circumstances giving rise to these arguments—namely, the spread of anti-Semitism, the Arab-Jewish conflict, and the hegemonic policies of numerous nation-states—may not altogether disappear in the foreseeable future, morality requires that we strive to abolish them.

I. Jewish Hegemony and the Right to National Self-Determination

The concept of the right to self-determination of ethnocultural groups has two distinct senses both in international law and in political philosophy. One refers to the right to self-rule and the other to the right of secession. Neither of these meanings implies the right of ethnocultural groups to sovereignty

---

Shamgar, according to whom "the existence of the State of Israel as the State of the Jewish People does not negate its democratic nature, just as the Frenchness of France does not negate its democratic nature" (EA 1/88, *Neiman v. Chairman of the Central Elections Committee for the Twelfth Knesset*, P.D. 42[4], 189 [Hebrew]).

[9] An important example is A. B. Yehoshua's essay "Between Right and Right: One Right and Another," in A. B. Yehoshua, *Between Right and Right*, trans. Arnold Schwartz (Gar-den City, NY: Doubleday, 1981), 75–106.

nor to hegemony within a framework of their own nation-state. The right to self-rule can be implemented by granting the members of an ethnocultural group autonomy in particular domains of their lives, such as education or status (personal-substantive autonomy), or by granting them autonomy in a territory in which they enjoy exclusive or majority presence (territorial autonomy). Similarly, a group's right to secede from an existing state and to establish an independent state does not imply that this group necessarily has a right to hegemony and sovereignty over this new state. The right to secede can be justified in terms of the right to escape persecution and other types of injustice inflicted by the state from which a group has decided to secede; it need not necessarily be interpreted in terms of the right to establish ethnocultural hegemony in the new state.[10] These considerations indicate that the hegemonic interpretation of the right to self-determination does not necessarily follow from the meaning of this right in either of its senses (namely, the right to secede and the right to self-government). However, this does not mean that the hegemonic statist interpretation is not a possible interpretation or the appropriate interpretation of that right. In order for it to be the appropriate interpretation, one must show that the justifications for the right to self-determination provide greater support for this particular interpretation than they do for other interpretations. It must also be shown that considerations weighing against such an interpretation do not override those in its support. My argument will be that the justifications of the right to self-determination do not dictate the statist interpretation. On the other hand, the arguments against the statist interpretation are conclusive and prevail over the considerations in its support.

Arguments against the Statist Conception

There are several considerations that inveigh against the statist conception. The first and most important of these relates to the intrastate injustice caused by the realization of this version of self-determination. In the geodemographic conditions of most parts of the world, the realization of the statist conception in effect creates two classes of citizens, namely, citizens to whom the state can be said to belong and citizens who are, as it were, the state's subtenants. This inherent inequality has always figured prominently in the Israeli discourse regarding the Jewishness of the state and also in the discourse about Zionism since its early days. The fact that the hegemonic

---

[10] For a comprehensive philosophical discussion of the right to self-determination and the right to secession, see Allen Buchanan, *Justice, Legitimacy, and Self-Determination: Moral Foundations for International Law* (New York: Oxford University Press, 2004), part 3.

conception of Jewish self-determination implies unequal status for the Arabs has always been acknowledged in this discourse. Inevitably, it renders the Arabs living in the Jewish state outsiders in their own homeland. It is a well-known fact that most of the populations inhabiting territories in which states could possibly be formed do not enjoy national homogeneity. Under these circumstances, the aforementioned criticism applies to many nations which exercise hegemony within the states in which they realize their right to self-determination. Examples include Slovakia with its Hungarian minority, Macedonia with its Albanian minority, and the Ukraine with its Romanian minorities. Quite obviously, there are many other cases.[11]

A second important consideration for rejecting the hegemonic interpretation of the right to self-determination relates to the injustice it causes on the global level. Because of the geodemographic conditions of the world, the implementation of this conception means that not all nations can have states of their own or the special international status which is currently granted only to states. Unlike intrastatist injustice, the global injustice does not merely result from the fact that the populations of most territories in which states could be formed are of mixed ethnocultural origin, but also from the fact that many national groups do not have exclusive or majority presence within a territory in which a state could be established. The paradigmatic but by no means exclusive examples of this type of group are the indigenous peoples in America and Australia, where European settler states were created. Additional examples abound in Russia and in various parts of Asia, Africa, and Europe. The states in which these indigenous and other minority groups live perceive themselves as the nation-states of the groups constituting the majority, giving rise to inequality between these groups and the minority groups living among them. The inequality is inherent in the minority group's status within the state, in its relations with the majority group, and in its international status.

In the context of the Israeli-Palestinian conflict, the global inequality created by the statist conception carries somewhat less weight. This is because many participants in the debate on the solution maintain that, if Israel regards itself as a hegemonic nation-state belonging to the Jewish people, then there

---

[11] These include Estonia with its Russian minority, Bulgaria with its Turkish minority, Romania with its Hungarian minority, and Azerbaijan with its Armenian minority. In the not so distant past, it also applied to Spain with respect to the Catalans and to New Zealand with respect to the Māoris. However, the latter countries have adopted federal frameworks that now accommodate their homeland minorities.

should also be a Palestinian nation-state. Then, even if Palestinian citizens of Israel do not have equal status within the Israeli state context, the Palestinians as a nation would not suffer from inequality in the global arena. In the context of the Israeli-Palestinian conflict, it is urgent to bring an end to the injustice caused by the fact that the Palestinians do not have their own state, while Israel defines itself as an exclusively Jewish state. Given the urgent need to bring an end to this particular injustice, it is inappropriate to argue about the global injustice generally caused by the statist conception of self-determination. Nevertheless, this global injustice should not be ignored. Since not all ethnocultural groups can have states of their own, on a global level, the adoption of the statist conception necessarily creates two classes of ethnocultural groups, namely, those that have a state and those that do not.[12]

As far as possible, rights should be interpreted and implemented in a manner that ensures their equal allocation to all persons/groups. Ethnocultural groups' right to self-determination can either be interpreted as a right to which all ethnocultural groups are entitled or as the exclusive right of ethnocultural groups that are living in their homelands (therefore excluding immigrant groups).[13] Now, even if the right to self-determination is granted only to the latter category, its interpretation as a right to hegemony within the framework of a nation-state effectively precludes its equal allocation to all ethnocultural groups living in their homelands, inasmuch as there may be more than one ethnocultural group with ties to the same homeland. Admittedly, the right to self-determination can be further restricted to apply exclusively to ethnocultural groups that constitute a majority in their homelands. Indeed, the particular interests

---

[12] One could, of course, challenge the argument according to which one should not grant the right to statist self-determination to any ethnocultural groups because it is not possible to grant a statist right to self-determination to all ethnocultural groups. It could be argued that this is similar to claiming that, since it is impossible to give a particular kind of medication to all of the people who need it, no one should receive it. However, I do not think that the analogy between self-determination and medication is justified. I discussed this matter at greater detail in Gans, *The Limits of Nationalism*, 74–78.

[13] Obviously, there are groups which cannot be easily classified into any of these categories. Are the Russians living in the Baltic states also living in their homeland? They are certainly not immigrants. They were brought there at a time when these states were part of their homeland, namely, the Soviet Union. Are the Indo-Fijians living in their homeland? Certainly not in the sense that the native Fijians live in Fiji. But neither are they immigrants. They were brought to Fiji by the British. The same applies to African Americans in the United States. In my view, one must treat these groups as homeland groups. However, the substantiation of this position is not within the scope of this book.

that justify the rights of homeland groups to self-determination have yet to be clarified. Prima facie, however, it is difficult to conceive of any justified interpretation of these interests that could be exclusively applicable to ethnocultural groups that constitute the majority in their homelands, as distinct from the interests of other ethnocultural groups that are minorities in their homelands.

In sum, the hegemonic conception of the right to self-rule precludes the equal allocation of this right to all ethnocultural groups. In the world's current geodemographic conditions, the implementation of this conception creates injustice on the domestic level among the different groups living in the same state and injustice on the global scale among ethnocultural groups that have states and those that do not.

The Statist Interpretation and Justifications of the Right to Self-Determination

The statist conception of the right to self-determination or self-rule of ethnocultural groups has additional shortcomings. Apart from the problems it creates in the global and domestic spheres, it may be problematic from the perspective of the ethnocultural groups that enjoy it, and it is indeed problematic from the perspective of the values of pluralism and freedom of movement in the world. However, I will refrain from discussing these problems here.[14] Conceivably, one could challenge the practical or even moral significance of the aforementioned shortcomings of the statist conception if this conception were the only one satisfying the interests that justify the right to self-determination. However, one is hard put to argue convincingly that this is indeed the case. Ethnocultural groups have a right to self-determination that derives from their members' interest in adhering to their ancestors' culture, in leading their lives within the framework of their culture, and in preserving the multigenerational dimension of their culture. This is a universal right based on the fact that the interests justifying it are interests currently shared by many of the members of all ethnocultural groups. Most of the people living today desire to assure the continued existence of their particular culture and their ability to live their lives within the framework of their culture. It is important for their well-being, since their various choices and endeavors are meaningful only or at least primarily within this culture. Most people

---

[14] I discuss this elsewhere; see Gans, *The Limits of Nationalism*, chap. 3.

living today need to know that their culture will probably continue to exist and thrive. Hopelessness about the continued existence of their culture might easily undermine their faith in the meaningfulness of their own endeavors.[15] The right to national self-rule purports to serve the interests that people have in adhering to their culture and in preserving it for generations.

The interests referred to here are fundamental human interests. The right to self-rule is important both because it protects these interests and because the recognition of this right has significant implications for the world's political structure. However, there is nothing requiring that these interests be protected exclusively within the framework of a nation-state. The collective experience of many groups in the world indicates that the existence of a state is not the only framework that ensures the conditions for the protection and promotion of the fundamental interests referred to above. The French- and Flemish-speaking populations of Belgium; the French-, German-, Italian-, and Romansch-speaking populations in the various Swiss cantons; the Francophones and Anglophones in Canada; and the Maharashtrians, Tamils, and Bengalis of India all constitute concrete proof of this point. Of course, the cases of Bosnia and Lebanon should also be mentioned in this context as possible counterexamples, since their homeland ethnocultural groups have recently been in conflict. This also applies to the Jews and the Palestinians in the Land of Israel/Palestine. I shall discuss this case in the following section.

It is important to note that many contemporary writers who argue that the nation-state is the *desirable* means for protecting people's interests in self-determination do not also argue that it is a *necessary* means for achieving this goal. At most, they consider it to be the optimal means for self-determination. They argue that multinational states provide less protection for the various ethnocultural groups living within them than would be accorded by separate nation-states for each one of these groups.[16] However, I am not certain if this latter claim is correct. The determination of the optimal means for protecting people's interests in their nationality and the right to self-determination depends on many different variables, such as the size and the wealth of the group concerned, its ability to adapt itself to ever-changing circumstances, the extent to which members

---

[15] For a detailed discussion of all of these points, see ibid., chap. 2.

[16] See David Miller, *On Nationality* (Oxford: Clarendon, 1995), chap. 4.

of the group are committed to it and to its culture, and the nature of the other ethnocultural groups that live in close proximity to the group concerned. There is therefore little point in making generalizations, and each case should preferably be addressed individually. However, even if it were true, either in general or with respect to a particular case, that the nation-state is indeed the optimal means for the protection of people's interests in living within the framework of their ethnocultural group, there are two points that would still require emphasis. First, nonoptimal means may nonetheless be sufficient for the attainment of the intended goals. Second, even if the nation-state may indeed be the optimal means for satisfying people's interests in their national culture, it must be noted that people have other interests as well. People's interests in being treated with respect and as equals are interests of no less importance than their interests in adhering to their culture, living within it, and sustaining it for generations. Adopting the statist interpretation of self-determination may indeed serve the interests of many people in their culture, but may also violate the interests of many others in being treated with respect and as equals. If this is indeed the case, the statist interpretation of self-determination should be rejected.

A Substatist Interpretation of the Right to Self-Determination

Instead of the statist interpretation of the right to self-determination, it would be more appropriate to interpret self-determination as a sub- and interstatist right. According to this interpretation, the constitutional relationship between ethnocultural nations and the states in which they enjoy self-determination should not be one of sovereignty over the state or "ownership" of the state. Rather, each ethnocultural group and all those belonging to it should be granted a package of privileges within the state that extends over the territory of their homeland. This package should include self-government rights, special representation rights, and cultural preservation rights.[17] *Self-government rights* include powers and liberties that allow members of a national group to shape their culture and substantial parts of their lives within its framework. *Representation rights* are rights guaranteeing the group a fair share in the government and in the symbols of

---

[17] It could be claimed that international law provides a certain degree of support for the current position. International law distinguishes between internal self-determination of ethnocultural groups, that is, their power to manage their own affairs by themselves, and

the state. *Cultural preservation rights* are auxiliary rights and other means for protecting the group members' ability to shape their culture independently and to live their lives within it. In order to preserve their culture, cultural groups require special rights and other means in order to maintain a sufficiently large population in their territorial homeland (or in parts of the territorial homeland, which may decrease in size if their population decreases in numbers), thus allowing them to maintain their culture as the dominant culture in the public sphere.[18]

This conception is substatist because the rights under discussion are rights *within* the framework of a state rather than rights *to* a state or to independent statehood. Therefore, they are rights that could in principle be enjoyed by more than one national group within the framework of any one state. These rights are based on the interests that all members of an ethnonational group—including those members of an ethnonational group living in the diaspora—might have in their nationality, and not only on the interests of those who are citizens of the state. This is part of what makes the present conception interstatist.

The rights included within the sub- and interstatist conception of national self-determination should be allocated equally among all ethnocultural groups within the framework of the states governing their homelands. The condition of equal allocation is one which ethnocultural groups must and can indeed fulfill under the sub- and interstatist conception of national self-determination. This is not the case when the right to self-determination is interpreted under the statist conception. The rights included within the sub- and interstatist conception must of course also be subject to constraints deriving from the basic human rights to freedom, dignity, and subsistence. Thus, these rights cannot, for example, permit national groups to limit the birthrates of nonmembers in the territories in which they enjoy self-government nor to expel them from these territories.

The sub- and interstatist conception of national self-determination does not suffer from the shortcomings of the statist conception.[19] It is impossible to apply the latter in an equal and universal manner because of the limited

---

external self-determination, which means the right to secede from an existing state and to establish a new one. Since the 1990s, in the wake of the dissolution and disintegration of the Soviet Union and Yugoslavia, international law has attributed greater importance to internal self-determination than to external self-determination.

[18] For a more detailed discussion, see Gans, *The Limits of Nationalism*, chap. 3.

[19] For a more detailed discussion of this subject, see ibid., 85–90.

territorial resources of the world, its stability requirements, the needs that states are supposed to satisfy, and factors related to the world's ethnocultural geodemography. This shortcoming is not shared by the substatist conception. The package of rights comprising the right to self-determination under this conception can be equally allocated among all ethnocultural groups, irrespective of their size and of whether they constitute the majority or a minority in a given territory. Universal implementation of the substatist and interstatist conception thus prevents the global injustice caused by the statist conception. The implementation of the substatist conception would not ascribe moral value to empirical inequalities that exist between national groups. It would not doom individuals around the world to inferiority merely because they belong to stateless ethnocultural groups. However, it must be noted that, at least prima facie, the implementation of the sub- and interstatist conception would fail to redress the domestic injustices caused by the statist conception. The statist conception creates two classes of citizens, namely, those who enjoy the rights to ethnocultural self-determination in a given state and those who live in the same state but do not enjoy these rights. The substatist conception would not create these two classes with regard to citizens belonging to ethnocultural groups that are also homeland groups within the state.[20] However, it would create distinctions between citizens belonging to a given country's homeland groups and those who do not belong to such groups (for example, members of immigrant groups or of groups that view themselves as living in exile from their homelands).

Nonetheless, supporters of ethnocultural groups' right to self-determination and self-government need not regard this shortcoming as a problem, because the inequality in citizenship sanctioned by the sub- and interstatist conception stems from the fact that the self-determination of ethnocultural groups should be in their respective homelands.[21] Homelands play a central role in defining the identities of almost all national groups in the world. The domestic inequality created by the sub- and interstatist conception is therefore essentially different from the domestic inequality that results from the statist

---

[20] In other words, I am referring to native ethnocultural groups, that is, to homeland and indigenous groups in the broad sense of these terms, including settlers who became a nation within the territories of the state and who regard the state as their homeland (for example, the Francophones and Anglophones in Canada), and exiles who continue to regard the territories left by their ancestors thousands of years ago as their homeland and who have not established any other homeland, such as the Jews and their connection to the Land of Israel.

[21] See chapter 2.

conception. The latter makes moral distinctions on the basis of majority or minority membership, which is irrelevant to people's interest in their nationality. In contrast, the sub- and interstatist conception makes moral distinctions on the basis of homeland or nonhomeland membership. This distinction is inherently relevant to people's interest in their cultural nationality.

The nature of the sub- and interstatist conception proposed here can be illuminated by referring to the recent debate in Israel as to whether Israel is a *Jewish state, the state of the Jews,* or *the state of the Jewish people.* This debate echoes the debates that have accompanied Zionist thinking since its inception. Relying on no less an authority than Theodor Herzl, there are those who claim that Israel should not be described as a *Jewish state,* but rather as *the state of the Jews.* What they mean is that the description should be no more than an empirical description of the state as one in which Jews constitute the majority.[22] Presumably, they would also argue that the existence of a Jewish majority in the State of Israel constitutes the sole moral basis (because of the democratic principle of majority rule) for the status of Hebrew as its official language, as well as for the Jewish character of its festivals and other symbols. Accordingly, if there were not a Jewish majority in Israel, the Jews would not be entitled to their current predominant presence in the public sphere of the state.

On the other hand, those who view Israel as a *Jewish state* and not just *the state of the Jews* intend to stress that Israel's Jewish character is not merely the result of the demographic fact that the Jews constitute the majority population in the state. Rather, they maintain that the Jews as an ethnocultural group should enjoy privileges in Israel irrespective of whether they are a majority in the state or not (although many of the writers whose works I have read on this issue seem to deliberately avoid using the term "privileges" in this context). The privileges in question include, inter alia, the right of the Jewish ethnocultural group to adopt at least certain measures other than natural reproduction in order to ensure that they remain a majority within Israel. Proponents of the view that the state should be described as a *Jewish state* also believe that the state's various symbols and its national anthem should be exclusively Jewish. They argue further that, in addition to utilizing the state for the exclusive benefit of the Jews, the Jews are entitled to define the state as an entity that belongs to the entire Jewish

---

[22] See citations from Mordechai Bar-On in Yoram Hazony, "Did Herzl Want a 'Jewish' State?" *Azure* 9 (2000), 40.

nation, including its diaspora, and not just to those Jews actually living in Israel.[23] These additional privileges are generally interpreted as an expression of the right to a Jewish nation-state, which means the Jewish people's right to a state of its own. In distinguishing between the concept of a *Jewish state* and the concept of *the state of the Jews*, Ruth Gavison notes: "A Jewish state is a state in which the Jewish people realizes its right to self-determination, or in other words, Israel is the nation-state of the Jewish people."[24]

Those who claim that Israel ought to be described as *the state of the Jewish people* express ideas similar to those who view Israel as a *Jewish state*. The difference, if any, is that those who describe Israel as *the state of the Jewish people* emphasize the fact that Israel should not limit these special privileges to the Jews residing in it but should also grant them to the Jewish diaspora. In other words, they mean that Israel is the nation-state of *all* Jews, not just Israeli Jews.[25]

By resorting to the sub- and interstatist interpretation of the right to self-determination, one could concur with the first part of Gavison's assertion, namely, that a *Jewish state* is a state in which the Jewish people exercises its right of self-determination. At the same time, it is also possible to disagree with the second part of her assertion, namely, that the

---

[23] As noted above, my impression is that the proponents of the hegemonic interpretation of the Jewish state are afraid to speak openly about special privileges for Jews. This impression is based on the fact that they actually demand such privileges while simultaneously denying that this is indeed what they are demanding. For one example, see Yakobson and Rubinstein, *Israel and the Family of Nations*, 8. In addition, Yoram Hazony states, "Israel had been established as a 'Jewish state,' not only in terms of its demographics, but also in its purpose, values, policies and institutions" (Hazony, "Did Herzl Want a 'Jewish' State?" 40). Again, there is no explicit mention here of special privileges, but this is certainly what Hazony's comments boil down to.

[24] Ruth Gavison, *Can Israel Be Both Jewish and Democratic: Tensions and Prospects* (Jerusalem: Van Leer Institute, Hakibbutz Hameuchad, 1999), 26 (Hebrew).

[25] The Knesset used the concept of *the state of the Jewish people* in 1985 when it added section 7A to the Basic Law: The Knesset, 1958. This section allows the disqualification of political parties that have a racist platform and of political parties that deny Israel's right to exist as the state of the Jewish people. This section of the law has been amended over the years and today requires the disqualification of parties which deny Israel's right to exist as a Jewish and democratic state. However, the expression *the state of the Jewish people* was also used in the amendment to section 1A(1) of the Immunity of Members of Parliament Law (Rights and Duties), 1951, passed in 2002. The Knesset's use of *the state of the Jewish people* in its amendment of the Basic Law: The Knesset, 1958 was the result of a proposal made by Member of Knesset Elazar Granot of the socialist Mapam Party. Granot's intention was to avoid using the phrase *Jewish state* with its national religious innuendo in Israeli political discourse. The definition of the concept of *the state of the Jewish people* was supposed to express the fact that Israel was established in order to exercise the Jewish people's right to its own state (Yakobson and Rubinstein, *Israel and the Family of Nations*, 199; for a detailed discussion of this terminological debate,

right to self-determination is synonymous with the right to a nation-state.[26] By means of the sub- and interstatist conception, one could also reject the idea expressed by the proponents of the view that Israel should be described as *the state of the Jews* merely by virtue of its Jewish majority. However, acceptance of the sub- and interstatist conception precludes the notions that self-determination should be enjoyed by Jews only or that self-determination should be used as a justification for Jewish hegemony. The sub- and interstatist conception makes it possible for us to share the belief held by many Jews that Jewish ethnocultural self-determination in Israel is the realization of the right to self-determination of the entire Jewish people and not only of that part of the nation living in Israel. However, in principle at least, it implies that this relationship with members of the nation living in the diaspora is not unique to Jews. In other words, the sub- and interstatist conception of the right to self-determination proposed here does not commit one to interpreting the right to Jewish self-determination in Israel as a right to a hegemonic nation-state, a right to Jewish exclusivity in the symbols of the state, its festivals, and its methods of legal interpretation, or even as the right to continue maintaining a majority. Yet it does entail an interpretation of this right to self-determination as consisting of several privileges which must be enjoyed by Jews, though not only by Jews. According to this interpretation, Jews may indeed enjoy privileges in Israel with respect to the symbols of the state, its festivals, and the right to

see pp. 195–204, this volume). I interpret the phrase *the state of the Jewish people* as stressing that Israel constitutes the realization of the self-determination of the whole Jewish people and not only of the Jews residing in Israel. This is the way the phrase was interpreted by critics who questioned the idea underlying this phrase. They were against the notion that "the State of Israel is the state of all the Jews in the world who are not its citizens, but it is not the state of some of its citizens [i.e., its Arab citizens]," per Azmi Bishara, cited in Yakobson and Rubinstein, *Israel and the Family of Nations*, 199. See ibid. for similar citations of Baruch Kimmerling and Shulamit Aloni. However, it is important to note that many of those who use the phrase *Jewish state* (Gavison, Yakobson and Rubinstein, Hazony, and writers along almost the entire political spectrum in Israel, from the Zionist Left to the radical Right) believe that Israel is the state of the entire Jewish people, to the same extent as those who use the phrase *the state of the Jewish people*.

[26] In her article "The Jews' Right to Statehood: A Defense," Gavison states that the right to self-determination also admits of the substatist interpretation, in addition to its statist interpretation. She does not repeat the assertion that self-determination is synonymous to having a nation-state. However, this did not prevent her from justifying the Jewish nation-state by resorting to the right to national self-determination while ignoring the arguments against the statist interpretation of this right in general and specifically those that pertain to the Jewish state.

immigrate to Israel. Specifically, these privileges include the right to be represented in the state's symbols, for public life to be conducted in such a way that will ensure the preservation of Jewish culture, and the implementation of measures that allow Jews to live in Israel in numbers sufficient for their culture to thrive. However, these additional rights do not mean exclusivity, nor do they require hegemony or a Jewish majority. Rather, these are collective privileges granted to those citizens of states who belong to homeland groups as opposed to citizens who are not members of those groups. However, it must be remembered that the Jews are not the only homeland group in Israel; the Palestinians also constitute a homeland group.

The upshot of these arguments is that the mere right to national self-determination does not provide a basis for Israel's hegemonic interpretation of its Jewishness. But, as intimated at the beginning of this chapter, in the public debate over the Jewishness of the State of Israel, supporters of the hegemonic interpretation resort to three additional arguments to substantiate their position. First, they invoke the fact that there are states all over the world that regard themselves as hegemonic nation-states even though their populations consist of more than one homeland group. Second, they resort to the history of the Jews and to the history of their persecution as a people. Finally, reference is made to the violent history of the Israeli-Palestinian conflict. My own view is that the third argument provides the best justification for the hegemonic conception in the Jewish Israeli context. However, its validity is circumstantial and not principled and, as I will demonstrate below, is subject to many qualifications.

2. THE PREVALENCE OF NATION-STATES, THE PERSECUTION OF THE JEWS, AND THE ISRAELI-PALESTINIAN CONFLICT

The Prevalence of Nation-States

In *Israel and the Family of Nations: Jewish Nation-State and Human Rights*,[27] authors Alexander Yakobson and Amnon Rubinstein address issues similar to the problems dealt with in this book. Yakobson and Rubinstein attempt to show that there are many countries all over the world in which ethno-cultural hegemony has been institutionalized in a fashion similar to that of the Israeli case. They cite such countries as Greece, Germany, Finland,

---

[27] Yakobson and Rubinstein, *Israel and the Family of Nations*.

and Hungary, all of which implement policies of ethnic hegemony. In most of these countries, the institutionalization of the dominant group's ethno-cultural hegemony is manifested inter alia by the emphasis placed on the links of the state with the diaspora of the group, immigration or citizenship privileges granted to diaspora members of the ethnically hegemonic group, and the unique political status granted to the group's particular religion. Yakobson and Rubinstein's many examples imply the popular "everybody does it" argument in support of the hegemonic concept. Even Michael Walzer invokes this argument in his review of Chomsky's book *Peace in the Middle East?* conceding, "Arabs [are] cut off from whatever sense of Jew-ishness is fostered by the Israeli state." "But," he continues, "this is true of national minorities throughout the world. . . . Arab immigrants to France, for example, are cut off from whatever sense of Frenchness is fostered by the state."[28] Ruth Gavison too admits that Jewish ethnocultural hegemony in Israel sentences the Arabs living in Israel to feelings of alienation and to inequality, but claims that this is not unique to Israel; she notes that Jews in the United States, for example, share a similar fate:

> The overwhelming majority of the citizens of the United States is numeri-cally and culturally Christian. Christianity is a part of the self-definition of most Americans and of the self-perception of the state, despite the official separation of church and state. Unquestionably, this creates a situation in which actively identifying Jews feel a certain feeling of estrangement, of a belonging which is less than complete. [However,] problems of belonging and identity exist in all states.[29]

These analogies are of questionable validity. Gavison and Walzer must surely be aware of the distinction between homeland minorities, such as the Arabs in Israel, Corsicans in France, and Native Americans in the United States, on the one hand, and the immigrant minorities to which they refer, such as Jews in the United States and Arabs in France. They must also real-ize that France's policies toward Corsicans and America's policies toward Native Americans were either criticized or were significantly different from Israel's policies toward its homeland Arab minority. Even with regard to immigrant minorities or similar groups, such as foreign workers from the Philippines, South America, Africa, and Romania, Israel's treatment of these

---

[28] *New York Times Book Review* (October 6, 1974), 6. Walzer repeated an identical claim and the French analogy in a more recent exchange with Tony Judt regarding the possibility of turning Israel into a binational state. See *New York Review of Books* (December 4, 2003), 57.

[29] Gavison, *Can Israel Be Both Jewish and Democratic*, 39.

groups is less accommodating than the French and American treatment of similar groups. While the latter countries expel illegal immigrants, they also have institutionalized practices which allow legal immigration and the integration of immigrant minorities within their nations. Israel, on the other hand, expels non-Jews or those who lack kinship ties with Jews and is absolutely unwilling to even consider their institutionalized naturalization and integration. Yakobson and Rubinstein provide a far richer range of examples than those cited by Gavison and Walzer which allegedly show that "everybody does it." However, like Gavison's and Walzer's examples, those cited by Yakobson and Rubinstein also do not legitimize Israeli practices. For example, Yakobson and Rubinstein refer to Greece's preferential immigration policy toward ethnic Greeks. Yet Greece does not deny naturalization rights to people who are not of Greek ethnic origin. Another example mentioned by Yakobson and Rubinstein is Hungarian legislation that grants special rights to members of the Hungarian diaspora. However, they fail to mention that this legislation has been harshly criticized both inside and outside Hungary. The same applies to special immigration and citizenship rights conferred by Germany to ethnic Germans. These rights were never granted to all members of the ethnic nation, as is the case in Israel. They were restricted to ethnic Germans who suffered persecution as a result of World War II or as a result of the fall of the communist bloc. Americans of German origin have never enjoyed special immigration rights to Germany. Moreover, Germany recently liberalized its naturalization laws with regard to immigrants who are not ethnic Germans by mixing its traditional *jus sanguinis* principle of naturalization with elements of the *jus soli* principle. According to the former principle, citizenship is granted to descendants of those who are already citizens. The latter principle stipulates that citizenship should be granted to people born within the territory of the state.

I do not intend to reject the empirical validity of the claim that Israel is not alone in its ethnocultural bias by analyzing examples such as these in detail.[30] In certain matters, the extent of Israel's ethnocultural bias is indeed without precedent, while in others it is not. In chapter 5, I will undertake a detailed analysis of the justification for some specific examples. In this chapter, however, I will evaluate the general nature of the "everybody does

---

[30] One example must be mentioned here: In legislating Israel's perception of itself as a *Jewish state* or as the *state of the Jewish people*, the State of Israel has failed to add that it is also the state of its citizens who do not belong to the Jewish people. On the other hand, in the constitutions of Serbia, Croatia, and Macedonia, while they declare that they are the

it" argument and the nature of the legitimacy that it could confer on Israel's bias in favor of Jews.

It must be stressed that "everybody does it" is an apologetic argument usually invoked in order to justify something which is unjust and is usually not invoked in order to justify something which is just in its own right. The natural response to the question of why one does not give or take bribes would presumably be "because bribery is prohibited" and not "because most people don't give or take bribes." It is only people who occasionally indulge in bribery who might excuse themselves by arguing that "everybody takes bribes." It thus becomes clear why the ubiquity of the hegemonic nation-state is so frequently invoked by those attempting to justify Israel's hegemonic interpretation of its right to self-determination. Since this interpretation is not justified on its own merit, its proponents are forced to argue that many other peoples also interpret their right to self-determination in a similar way. The fact that a particular act is widely practiced may occasionally provide a justification for it. In other cases, it is nothing more than an excuse for committing this act, while in yet others it functions as a gauge to measure the severity of new acts (and often the character of the offenders). For example, if I attempt to justify my own acts of littering or polluting public areas by pointing out that everybody does it, the general practice serves to justify my individual act. If most people pollute public areas, this means that the public domain will be polluted in any case, and my own contribution is therefore negligible.[31] Similarly, the fact that everyone drives on the right side of the road is certainly a justification for my doing so. In this example, the general practice is the justification for my own conduct, for it is important to establish a single unified practice (that is, all people driving on the same side). On the other hand, consider the case of officials who have made a practice of embezzling public monies. It would certainly not be valid to argue that this general practice justifies my own acts of embezzlement. The fact that "everyone else" embezzles public funds might be a reason for forgiving me for my own act of embezzlement, provided that the general custom had created a situation

---

nation-states of the Serbs, the Croatians, and the Macedonians, respectively, they also declare that they are the states of their citizens who are not members of these ethnic nations. See Robert M. Hayden, "Constitutional Nationalism in the Formerly Yugoslav Republics," *Slavic Review* 5 (1992), 654–673, especially 657.

[31] There are certain exceptions to this, but they are not important for the present argument. In any case, they are not within the scope of this book.

in which I had no other means of earning a living or if, because of the general custom, my financial situation was significantly worse than that of the majority of those surrounding me. It could even provide grounds for leniency in the evaluation of my character, even if I had an alternative way of making a living. I could claim that I am not a criminal by nature, but merely spineless.

Cases related to pollution or littering demonstrate that the realization of certain communal goals (in this example, a litter-free or clean public sphere) requires the cooperation of the entire community. This goal cannot be achieved without the cooperation of the public at large. If the number of people cooperating is relatively small, the public good will not be produced in any case, which means that there is no longer any reason for anyone to comply. Questions such as which side of the road to drive on belong to the class of coordination problems and are solved by conventions. The embezzlement example concerns acts which are inherently wrong, irrespective of the accepted norm. Even if the prevalence of acts belonging to this category may in certain cases excuse certain specific acts committed by specific people, it certainly does not justify them.

The hegemonic interpretation of the right to self-determination belongs to the third of the above categories. Many states do indeed interpret the right of their dominant ethnocultural groups to self-determination as a right to hegemony. This constitutes grounds for not being overly harsh in judging Israel for the fact that it follows suit. It may even provide a certain justification for the Jews to interpret their right to self-determination in this manner, but it is doubtful whether such justification is sufficient, and it certainly does not render the implementation of this interpretation completely legitimate. The statist interpretation of self-determination is wrong, because its implications are inherently wrong. As many writers have stressed, and as I reiterated above, implementing the statist conception of the right to self-determination creates inequality in the allocation of rights among homeland groups. In the case of Israel, the realization of the statist interpretation of the Jews' right to self-determination means denying the members of another homeland group full membership in the very state in which they live. Whether or not this is classified as an injustice does not depend on what other states or ethnocultural groups do. Each individual instance is independently and intrinsically wrong, and the proliferation of such actions does not justify committing additional acts belonging to the same category.

In any event, let's assume, for the sake of argument, that Israel's hegemonic interpretation of the right to Jewish self-determination is justified
because other states have acted similarly. It would be justified in either of
the two senses outlined above, namely, as in the claim that littering public
property is justified because everybody does it, or in the ameliorative sense
of presenting individual acts of embezzlement as less severe if embezzlement is the general norm. Both are cases of undesirable conduct which
should ultimately be eliminated. In other words, even if the "everybody
does it" argument renders Israel's hegemonic interpretation of Jewish self-
determination legitimate, ideally such legitimacy should be of limited dura-
tion. Rather, it is incumbent upon us to change the fact that hegemonic
nation-states currently constitute the norm.

Justice does not necessarily require, however, that Israel take the lead in
changing this undesirable practice. At least in this case, in view of the history of Jewish persecution and the history of the Jewish-Palestinian conflict
over Palestine/the Land of Israel, Israel need not necessarily be "a light unto
the nations."

The Persecution of Jews and the Jewish-Arab Conflict

In chapter 2, I discussed the important role that the persecution suffered
by Jews played in justifying Zionism and the establishment of the State of
Israel. Many people believe that the force of this justification has not waned.
Yakobson and Rubinstein's book contains 413 pages of examples drawn
from other countries to justify a hegemonic Jewish nation-state. Apparently sensing the inadequacy of these examples as a justification for Jewish
hegemony in Israel, they conclude their book with an additional 13 pages
devoted to persecution. Similarly, in her attempt to justify the Jewish hegemonic state, Gavison resorts to the traditional Zionist thesis that "the Jewish
state will solve the problems of security and peace experienced by the Jews
in their diaspora countries."[32]

Some versions of the persecution argument assume that the kind of
persecution that justifies self-determination is that which is specifically
characteristic of the Jews, namely, persecution due to anti-Semitism, while
others suppose that being the victim of persecution is a phenomenon

---

[32] Gavison, *Can Israel Be Both Jewish and Democratic*, 55. In a well-known presentation of
the persecution argument, A. B. Yehoshua claims: "The Jewish People has a full moral right to
seize *part* of Eretz Yisrael or of *any other land*, even by force, on the basis of ... the survival right
of the endangered" (Yehoshua, "Between Right and Right," 78).

endemic to the condition of being a nation without a state and is thus also experienced by many other nations. Another variety concerns the reasons that the persecution argument constitutes a justification for the establishment of a nation-state. Is the nation-state justified because it guarantees the physical security of a persecuted nation, or because it grants a measure of dignity to the victims of persecution? Inevitably, each possible answer gives rise to additional questions. Those who believe that persecution specifically motivated by anti-Semitism justifies a Jewish nation-state disagree on the nature of anti-Semitism. Specifically, is anti-Semitism a cosmic decree or an irreversible law of nature and history? Or perhaps it is the product of historical contingencies, meaning that it might eventually disappear?[33] Those contending that it is not specifically the anti-Semitic persecution of the Jews that justifies a nation-state but rather the persecution experienced by many stateless nations could be divided over whether the lack of a state means the lack of a homeland, or whether it only means the lack of statehood in the homeland. Alternative interpretations as to why persecution justifies the establishment of a nation-state may themselves be the result of alternative answers to the question of why the nation-state removes the ignominy of persecution—either because it provides a national haven for endangered members of the nation in the diaspora, or because it means that there is a framework within which government-backed persecution is not possible, or a combination of the two. I will begin with the argument based on persecution as a general phenomenon characteristic of some stateless peoples.

As mentioned above, this argument admits of two interpretations, based on the ambiguity of the phrase "stateless peoples." According to one interpretation, such peoples lack a state in which they can exercise self-determination, even of the substatist type. As the Israeli writer A. B. Yehoshua notes, they are peoples without a homeland. His examples are the Armenians, the Gypsies, and the Jews in the nineteenth century and in parts of the twentieth century.[34] According to the second interpretation, "stateless" peoples are peoples that do not enjoy hegemonic sovereignty within the framework of their own state. This group is far larger than the first group, including inter alia the Catalans, the Francophones in Quebec, the Chechens, the Flemish, the Walloons, the Francophones in Switzerland, and the Inuit of Canada. The

---

[33] For a debate between A. B. Yehoshua and several others (mainly historians) concerning the origins of anti-Semitism, see *Alpayim* 28 (2005) (Hebrew).

[34] Yehoshua, "Between Right and Right," 99.

thesis that nations without a state are vulnerable to persecution seems to be plausible especially when referring to the first sense of statelessness, that is, with reference to nations which do not enjoy self-determination of any kind and are thus "homeless." It is far less plausible when applied to nations enjoying self-determination in their homelands, but to a degree less than statehood. The Jews and the Armenians were persecuted for as long as they did not enjoy any type of self-determination. The Gypsies are still experiencing persecution, perhaps because they still do not enjoy self-determination.

However, it is difficult to make the same claim with regard to the Catalans, the Quebecois, the Flemish, the French-speaking people of Wallonia, and most of the nations referred to above. The Chechens might be an exception. However, even in their case, it is difficult to ascribe their persecution to the fact that they do not have a state in which they enjoy hegemony and sovereignty. Their current persecution by the Russians resembles the way the Czechs were persecuted by the Germans in World War II, when they did enjoy a certain measure of sovereignty. The argument referring to the persecution of stateless peoples in general (as opposed to persecution due to anti-Semitism) could therefore be invoked to justify the Jewish right to a homeland and self-determination, but does not require a hegemonic nation-state. Furthermore, this conclusion is not exclusively based on a generalization from particular concrete cases but is also supported by general arguments. On the one hand, the substatist version of self-determination does grant limited political power to ethnocultural groups. On the other hand, the statist version of self-determination does not confer unlimited political power on ethnocultural groups. In other words, self-determination, whether hegemonic or nonhegemonic, only grants limited power to those enjoying it. Although it enhances their dignity, it cannot provide absolute physical security. By granting limited political power, self-determination provides the nation enjoying it with the means for self-defense, to be used when necessary. It may prevent situations in which people are exposed to the humiliation that characterizes persecution when they lack the ability to protect themselves. However, with regard to their ability to defend themselves, there is no difference between those who enjoy substatist self-determination and those who enjoy hegemony in the framework of a nation-state. There are obviously significant differences in the defensive capacities of different nations. But the differences in their defensive capacities are not the product of the specific type of self-determination that they might have exercised. Rather, their defensive capacity depends on the military and political strengths of the groups concerned, the strengths of their enemies, and similar variables.

That version of the persecution argument which specifically invokes anti-Semitism also admits of two interpretations, one of which regards the Jews as predestined to constant persecution while the other regards anti-Semitism as the product of unfortunate but contingent factors that may change in the future. With regard to the Jewish case, it could be argued that both interpretations at present justify making an exception to the general norm of realizing self-determination in a substatist manner. The latter of the above two interpretations could be argued to justify this exception because of the current manifestations of anti-Semitism, which have been particularly prominent since the beginning of the second intifada.[35] However, this justification is not particularly powerful, because the factors that made anti-Semitism a threatening phenomenon in the past are no longer as significant. As a minority, Jews have been vulnerable to religious persecution throughout history. They were the embodiment of "otherness" because of their religion, appearance, way of life, and customs. In the decades since World War II, the prominence of these factors has diminished drastically. On the one hand, this may be the result of the "normalization" of Jewish existence, which was one of the goals of Zionism, and the secularization and nationalization of Jewish life in contrast to the Jews' earlier life in the diaspora, which was mainly in religious communities. On the other hand, it could also be the result of general processes which continue to impact on political, cultural, and geodemographic conditions all over the world.

The Zionist movement has created a situation in which Jews now enjoy self-determination in a political framework that is essentially secular. However, due to global demographic changes, many other nations today have diaspora communities, and the Jews are no longer the only minority that represents otherness vis-à-vis their environment. In those countries formerly known for their anti-Semitism, Jewish otherness is now far less conspicuous. On the global level, interreligious antagonism has decreased significantly, at least in the context of Judeo-Christian relations. In addition, international law and human rights figure prominently in the political arena, certainly far more than they did in the past. Thus, although anti-Semitism does exist, it is often less blatant than it was in the past. Finally,

---

[35] The "second intifada" refers to the Palestinian uprising against the Israeli occupation of the Palestinian territories, which took place in the years 2000–2004.

it is important to mention the Holocaust and its lessons regarding the possible consequences of anti-Semitism and of all other forms of xenophobia.

The combination of all of these factors has reduced the overall threat posed by anti-Semitism, and as such, contemporary anti-Semitism no longer constitutes as compelling an argument for a statist interpretation of self-determination as it did in the 1930s and 1940s. Moreover, the justification for hegemony that anti-Semitism could provide is limited both in terms of the areas to which it can be applied and in terms of the time frame during which it can be said to be valid. Regarding the former, such hegemony should be restricted to the two areas of security and demography, for it is hegemony in these areas which could affect the safety and dignity of persecuted Jews. It does not justify hegemony in other areas, such as state symbols and education. Finally, anti-Semitism cannot be considered as a principled justification for hegemony. If it is a product of contingent factors, and since it is a phenomenon that morally should be abolished, it can only be interpreted as providing a circumstantial justification for hegemony and cannot be invoked to justify permanent hegemony.

However, if the justification for interpreting Jewish self-determination under the hegemonic conception is premised on a view of anti-Semitism as a permanent fixture in world history, then the position outlined above regarding the appropriate scope of hegemony must change with respect to whether or not hegemony should be permanent, but not with respect to the domains in which it is legitimate for it to be practiced. Anyone believing that history has chosen the Jews as eternal victims could not reasonably maintain that it is possible to guarantee their physical security. In this sense, it is irrelevant whether or not they enjoy self-determination, or whether or not they enjoy hegemony within their own state. Nonetheless, one could still believe that self-determination based on Jewish hegemony permanently increases Jews' control over their affairs and thus enhances their sense of dignity. If Jews are permanently threatened by persecution, as this interpretation of anti-Semitism implies, then there may be justification for hanging on to this means of defense and in refusing to waive it even temporarily. In such a case, it makes sense for the Jews to demand sole control over their security. A fortiori, it is not possible for them to share military organizations with the Arabs, who seem to be the main propagators of contemporary anti-Semitism. It is, however, important to stress that, even under the present interpretation of anti-Semitism and even if hegemony may not be limited in the temporal dimension, it should be limited in its scope and applied exclusively to the spheres of security and demography. This point is of particular importance given the assumption that the recent escalation in the Jewish-Arab conflict is either the reason for the emergence of contemporary anti-Semitism or the source of legitimacy for "that monster that refuses to die, which raises its head at every opportunity," to quote the cliché used by Yakobson and Rubinstein.[36] According to both explanations, the phenomenon of anti-Semitism requires reasons or at least excuses and opportunities for its resurgence. Within the Jewish-Palestinian dispute, the Jews must therefore fully comply with the demands and constraints of justice, not only because they *are* the demands and constraints of justice, but also so as not to provide reasons, excuses, and opportunities for the resurgence of anti-Semitism. Hence, the obligation to comply with the demands and constraints of justice is both moral and pragmatic.

This brings me to the final argument, which may also be the most powerful argument for the hegemonic conception of Jewish self-determination. The Jewish-Palestinian conflict justifies Jewish hegemony in Israel for reasons emerging from some general truisms or facts that also apply to the particular realities of this conflict. One well-known truism is that relationships of trust between adversaries in disputes will generally not emerge unless the conflicts themselves are resolved and then, only after enough time has passed and the two parties have attempted to build such relationships. This may be said to be true irrespective of who was originally responsible for the conflict. In as much as this truism applies to all conflicts, it also pertains to the Jewish-Palestinian conflict. Second, the Jewish-Palestinian conflict is a dispute between two ethnocultural groups, namely, Israeli Jews, who as a group have realized the right to national self-determination for the whole Jewish people, and the Palestinians and, to a certain extent, all Arabs. I would like to stress that the Palestinians under discussion are not only those Palestinians living in the territories occupied by Israel since the Six-Day War and in the Palestinian diaspora, but also those Palestinians who are citizens of Israel. Admittedly, as Israeli citizens, their ability to actively participate in the conflict is both morally and practically constrained. However, in the context of this conflict, they often side with their ethnocultural group and not with the state in which they are citizens. As such, the dispute is between ethnocultural groups and not between states. Third, at least from the Israeli Jewish perspective, the

---

[36] See Yakobson and Rubinstein, *Israel and the Family of Nations*, 420. For similar comments, see Gavison, "The Jews' Right to Statehood," 75–77.

matters necessitating trust among Jews, Palestinians, and Arabs in general
are not minor issues, but rather impact the heart of the physical existence
of the Jews and their survival as a distinct society enjoying self-determination in the area between the Jordan River and the Mediterranean Sea.
Fourth, in the near future, the Jews in Israel may cease to be the majority
in the state. This is a source of considerable anxiety among Israeli Jews.
Moreover, the Jews are a small minority in the entire Middle East, while
Palestinian society is part and parcel of the ethnocultural makeup of the
entire region. This then is the reality: In view of the absence of trust
between Jews and Palestinians in matters of existential importance for the
Jews, and given the fact that the Jews are a minority in the region, the Jews
have good reason to believe that the Arabs in general and the Palestinians
specifically would ultimately not respect the Jewish people's interests in
their survival as a distinct society. As long as the conflict remains unre-
solved and as long as there are no relationships of trust among the parties,
the Jews must rely on their strength. In other words, they must continue to
live within the framework of a state within which they enjoy hegemony
and in which they have military power.

Even when an agreement which would end the current state of war
between the parties is reached, many years will have to pass before relations predicated on mutual trust can be established. Therefore, the position
held by most Israelis and, in fact, by the majority of those who have given
the conflict serious thought is that at least the first stage of the solution
of the conflict ought to be the establishment of two states in the territory
between the Jordan River and the Mediterranean Sea. A two-state solution
of this kind is required, inter alia, in order to reduce the injustice caused
by accommodating the Jewish interest in a hegemonic Jewish state, which
is currently justified. I refer here to the two categories of injustice identified earlier in the discussion of the hegemonic interpretation of the right
to self-determination, namely, the domestic injustice and global injustice
caused by the implementation of the statist conception. The existence of
an independent state in which Palestinians enjoy self-determination would
solve the problem of inequality in the normative status of Jews and Palestinians on the global level and would also reduce the number of Palestinians
living under conditions of domestic injustice. The establishment of two
states in the territory west of the Jordan River is also consistent with my
interpretation of the historical rights argument, as presented in chapter 2.
According to this interpretation, historical rights cannot be the basis for the
territorial sovereignty of ethnocultural groups and can only be the basis for

determining the geographical site where their right to self-determination ought to be realized.

The position advocating the establishment of two states between the Jordan River and the Mediterranean Sea as the first step toward resolving the Jewish–Palestinian conflict raises the well-known questions concerning the appropriate territorial division and the appropriate demographic division between the two states. I will deal with these questions in the next chapter. However, as noted above, the two-state solution would not totally solve the problem of domestic injustice in the state designated for Jewish self-determination. The reason is that the division of the relevant territory into two states, to be discussed in the next chapter, leaves a significant number of Palestinians in Israel, whereas Jews would continue to have hegemony in it. Needless to say, such hegemony should be subject to human rights constraints. Furthermore, the hegemonic Jewish state should also be permanently subject to the constraints deriving from the fact that its most serious justification originates in the Jewish–Arab conflict, and not in a principle that prescribes that the right to self-determination be realized in the form of a nation-state. The constraints in question are the ones mentioned above pertaining to both the areas to which Jewish hegemony can legitimately apply and the time frame that is acceptable for it. The hegemony in question would apply only to military power and the maintenance of a demographic majority and should be maintained in these areas only until a relationship of trust develops between the parties. These claims have moral implications for the constitutional, statutory, and other arrangements adopted by Israel in specific areas, such as immigration, land acquisition, state symbols, and language rights. These implications, especially in the area of immigration, will be discussed in chapter 5.

4

Dividing Up the Historical Homeland

At the end of the 1940s, when the Zionist aspiration to create a Jewish state in the Land of Israel seemed to be more justified than ever before, the idea of such a state also received international recognition: On November 29, 1947, the UN General Assembly passed a resolution to partition Palestine into two states, one of which would be Jewish and the other Arab. The Jews accepted the assembly's decision, though according to some historians their acceptance wasn't totally sincere.[1] However, the Arabs rejected the assembly's decision outright. A war thus erupted between the Jews and the Arabs within Palestine. After the Jewish state unilaterally declared its independence on May 14, 1948, several Arab armies invaded the country to join the Palestinian community in its fight against the State of Israel.[2] The war ended in a Jewish victory and a Palestinian catastrophe.

The final territorial division and the demographic distribution between Jews and Palestinians after this war differed from the partition in the UN resolution. The war gave rise to the 1949 ceasefire lines, which were Israel's borders until the Six-Day War in June 1967. These 1949 borders granted the Jews a larger area than the one allocated by the partition plan, while the Palestinian territory turned out to be smaller than the Palestinian area in the 1947 partition plan. The 1948 war also created the problem of the Palestinian refugees, who had fled from their homes in fear of the war or had

---

[1] Some members of the group known as the New Historians (see chapter 3, note 4) argue that Israel reached an unwritten agreement with King Abdullah of Jordan to divide the territory designated for the Palestinian state between them. See Avi Shlaim, *Collusion across the Jordan: King Abdullah, the Zionist Movement, and the Partition of Palestine* (New York: Columbia University Press, 1988); Ilan Pappé, *Britain and the Arab-Israeli Conflict 1948–51* (New York: St. Martin's, 1988).

[2] For a description of this war, see Benny Morris, *Righteous Victims: A History of the Zionist-Arab Conflict, 1881–2001* (New York: Vintage, 2001), chap. 5. On the question of the justifiability of the Arab resistance to the 1947 UN partition resolution, see chapter 2, note 33.

been expelled by the Jews.[3] Until the mid-1950s, many of these refugees attempted to return to their original homes within the ceasefire borders of Israel, but only a small minority succeeded. Using both legal measures and physical violence, Israel prevented the return of Arabs who had fled in 1948. It appropriated the property owned by these Arabs by means of legislation and thwarted their attempts to return to their original homes and properties by force.[4] In June 1967, in the wake of the Six-Day War, Israel captured territories west of the Jordan River and along the Mediterranean Sea which had not been under Israeli rule until that point. These territories—known as the West Bank and the Gaza Strip—and the huge Palestinian population living there have since remained under Israeli control. In addition, Israel has established many Jewish settlements in the occupied territories. Certain portions, such as East Jerusalem and the surrounding areas, have even been legally annexed, formally bringing them under Israeli sovereignty, at least as far as Israeli law is concerned.

For the purpose of the arguments presented in this book, none of these facts are in dispute. However, when conjoined with the position proposed at the end of the previous chapter—that the first step in solving the Jewish-Palestinian conflict is to establish two states between the Jordan River and the Mediterranean Sea—it is evident that the appropriate territorial and demographic divisions between the two political entities have very important implications concerning the justice of the contemporary political manifestation of Zionism. The main demographic issue is the problem of the 1948 refugees and their descendants. The main territorial issue is whether the division of the land should be based on the pre-1967 borders. The Palestinians appear to have accepted these borders in the sense that they are demanding Israel's withdrawal from all of the territories captured in 1967, but are not requiring that Israel withdraw from the pre-1967 borders to the territorial division of the 1947 partition plan.[5] Nonetheless, they are also making demands which seem to entail the undoing of the demographic consequences of the 1948 Israeli War of Independence. They

---

[3] Regarding the Palestinian flight in 1948 and their expulsion, see Benny Morris, *The Birth of the Palestinian Refugee Problem, 1947–1949* (Cambridge: Cambridge University Press, 1987).

[4] See Benny Morris, *Israel's Border Wars, 1949–1956: Arab Infiltration, Israeli Retaliation and the Countdown to the Suez War* (Oxford: Oxford University Press, 1997).

[5] This, at least, is the position of the Palestine Liberation Organization. Hamas seems to have a policy of remaining vague on this matter and sometimes officially denies Israel's right to exist as a state in which the Jewish people realizes its right to self-determination.

demand that Israel acknowledge the right of return of the 1948 refugees and their descendants to their original homes or near their original homes within the pre-1967 borders. On the other side, as stated above, all Israeli governments since 1967 have implemented a policy of settling and annexing areas beyond the 1967 borders. Since the early years of the State of Israel, all Israeli governments and an overwhelming majority of the Jewish public in Israel have objected to a mass return of Palestinian refugees into pre-1967 Israeli territory.

Opposition to the return of Palestinian refugees is even shared by the Zionist Left, which has been the most persistent Israeli proponent of a withdrawal to the 1967 borders. This position—calling for a withdrawal to the 1967 borders and also opposing the return of Palestinian refugees—has been challenged by many people in Israeli politics, both further to the right (namely, antiliberal nationalists) and further to the left (namely, the non- and anti-Zionist Left). These critics claim that the position of the Zionist Left is both logically and morally inconsistent. The pre-1967 borders and demographic distribution were the result of the expulsion of the Arabs during the 1948 war and the prevention of their return at the beginning of the 1950s. As such, so goes the argument, these borders are not morally superior to the post-1967 borders and current demographic reality, both of which are the result of Israel's settlement policy since 1967. The right wing in Israeli politics claims that, if the historical rights of the Jews and their right to self-determination justify the borders and demographic situation achieved by means of the 1948 war and the actions committed during this war (inter alia, the expulsion of hundreds of thousands of Palestinians), then they also justify the borders and demographic situation created in the aftermath of the 1967 war and the establishment of Jewish settlements on the West Bank. On the other hand, people whose political views are even further to the left than the Zionist Left, that is, the non- and anti-Zionist Left, claim that, if the borders and demographic situation that resulted from the 1967 war are not justified, then by the same token, there can be no justification for the borders and demography that resulted from the 1948 war and the expulsion of the Palestinians.

This chapter will discuss these issues. I will argue for a position that opposes a mass Palestinian return to the Jewish state and generally supports the pre-1967 borders as the basis for the borders of Israel. In section 1 of the chapter, I will discuss the issue of the Palestinian return. I will argue that, if the conclusion I reached in the last chapter is sound, namely, that the territories west of the Jordan River ought to be divided into two states, then it is morally appropriate to reject the claim that Israel's responsibility for creating the refugee problem should be acknowledged by allowing the refugees the right of *mass* return to their original places and to other places within the Jewish state. In section 2 of the chapter, I will deal with the question of whether the pre-1967 borders should constitute the basis for the borders of the Jewish state. After arguing for an affirmative answer to this question, I will show that there is no moral or logical inconsistency in a position that opposes the undoing of the demographic and territorial results of the 1948 war and, on the other hand, supports reversing the demographic and territorial results of the 1967 war. I will conclude the second half of this chapter with a few comments on two other issues which occasionally come up in Israel in debates over the demographic and territorial division of the territories west of the Jordan River. These are the questions of whether areas within the pre-1967 Israeli borders populated primarily by Palestinian citizens of Israel should be transferred to a Palestinian state and whether Israeli settlements established in the occupied territories after 1967 should be left within the future Palestinian state.

1. Demography and the Palestinian Right of Return

Anti-Zionist and Pro-Zionist Positions on a Mass Return of Palestinian Refugees

Even though it is appropriate for Israel to recognize its responsibility for the creation of the Palestinian refugee problem, it is both possible and appropriate to reject the demand that this responsibility be realized by allowing a mass return of the refugees to their original homes and to other places within the Jewish state. I contend that rejecting a mass return should even be acceptable to opponents of Zionism who define themselves as such because they are against the principle of the return of the Jews to Palestine.[6] If these opponents of Zionism can nonetheless reject a mass return of Palestinian refugees, so the argument would go, then a fortiori, supporters of Zionism in one form or another would certainly oppose such a return. But before I begin to argue for this claim, a few points are worth noting concerning those who advocate a mass return of Palestinian refugees.

---

[6] For this and other possible objections to Zionism, see chapters 1 and 2.

The position in favor of a mass Palestinian return could be held either by those who reject Zionism due to Arab chauvinism or ultranationalism or by those who reject Zionist ideology because they are antinationalist liberals or humanists. Arab chauvinists would probably support a mass return of Palestinian refugees and would perhaps also support the evacuation and expulsion of Jews to facilitate a return of Palestinian refugees. They would subscribe to such a position because, by definition, chauvinists consider their national group ontologically and morally to have priority over its individual members and a fortiori to have priority over individuals belonging to other national groups, and because they also assign decisive weight to the interests of their group as opposed to the interests of other groups. However, since chauvinism is generally a morally repugnant position, the same is necessarily true of Arab chauvinism. Arab chauvinism and its implications for the issue of the return of refugees can therefore be dismissed altogether.

Antinationalist liberals and humanists would probably support a mass return of Palestinian refugees to vacant areas in Israel. They would, however, reject uprooting and expelling individual Jews in order to allow this return. They would support a mass return to vacant places within the State of Israel because their antinationalist views preclude designating any particular area in the Land of Israel for the self-determination of any ethnocultural group. Furthermore, they would object to uprooting and expelling Jews. As liberals or humanists, they would aspire to restoring the status of individual refugees to their previous state so long as this does not adversely affect other individuals who are not responsible for the harm inflicted on the refugees. The position of antinationalist liberals should also be ignored here. However, it should certainly not be ignored for reasons of moral repugnance as in the case of Arab chauvinism but rather because of the problems facing the neutralist and the cosmopolitan interpretations of liberalism, which inform antinationalist liberals.[7] Moreover, with regard to the return of Palestinian refugees, the position of antinationalist liberals also lacks any practical significance. Within the intra-Israeli political discourse and that between Israelis and Palestinians, the controversy over the issue of the Palestinian return is not only whether it is appropriate to allow the return of refugees to their original homes, but also whether it is appropriate to allow them to return to those places *within the borders of the state that constitutes the realization of the Jewish right to self-determination*. Anyone rejecting nationalism

---

[7] For a detailed discussion, see chapter 1.

(or at least ethnocultural nationalism) in principle, including liberals, must also reject the right of ethnocultural groups to self-determination. This position, therefore, denies the fundamental presuppositions of the Israeli and the Israeli-Palestinian discourses concerning the right of return, and is therefore of no practical importance for the discussion in this chapter.

All other positions on Zionism, whether they belong to the anti-Zionist camp or support any one of the many versions of Zionist ideology, could object to a mass Palestinian return. I will now demonstrate this with regard to those who reject Zionism because they oppose the principle asserting the Jewish right to return to Palestine. As I noted in chapter 2, those who reject this Zionist principle do so because they believe that the fact that another ethnic group was living in the country at the time of the inception of Zionism constitutes a conclusive argument against the settlement of Jews in the Land of Israel.[8] This position could in principle be held both by liberal and nonliberal supporters of nationalism. My concern here is with the liberals. As liberals, their nationalism must be based on individual interests. Therefore, they necessarily attribute significant weight to the interests of the Jewish individuals who are currently living in Israel in continuing to live there and not be uprooted, regardless of the fact that their presence in Israel is the result of what they might consider Zionism's originally unjustified attempt to settle them there. These individual interests merit protection at least with respect to those individuals who are not responsible for the fact that they were born and raised in Israel.[9] Since these are significant interests, the liberal nationalist has no choice but to support the right of these individuals to remain in Israel, or at least must concede that there is no justification for expelling them. Furthermore, for the liberal nationalist, acknowledgment of the right of individual Jews currently living in Israel to continue living there also entails recognizing the right of these individual Jews—as a group—to self-determination in those territories in which they constitute the majority. In other words, liberal nationalists who believe that

---

[8] This is not the only argument they could make. They could also deny the factual claim that the Jews have some kind of connection to Palestine or the claim that it is of normative significance. But if my argument in chapter 2 is plausible, their most reasonable argument would be that, despite the Jews' meaningful connection with the Land of Israel, the fact that another population inhabited the country at the time of Zionism's inception constituted a conclusive reason against the realization of this connection.

[9] See Jeremy Waldron, "Superseding Historic Injustice," *Ethics* 103 (1992), 4–28, and "Settlement, Return and the Supersession Thesis," *Theoretical Inquiries in Law* 5 (2004), 237–268.

it was not justified for the Jews to return to the Land of Israel at the time of the inception of Zionism must nonetheless acknowledge that Jews who were either born in Israel or immigrated to Israel as infants and are not responsible for the fact that their lives are rooted there still have a moral right to national self-determination. Yet another way to put it is that, while liberal nationalism can logically reject Zionism, it nonetheless requires post facto acknowledgment of at least the normative consequences of a modest form of Zionism.[10] However, if it denies the justice of Zionist ideology and therefore also the justice of its concrete realization by the Zionist movement, then it can certainly hold the Zionist movement accountable for all the suffering incurred by Palestinian refugees.

The question that must therefore be addressed by liberal nationalists who are opposed to Zionism is whether this responsibility should be realized, inter alia, by means of the return of Palestinian refugees to their original homes or to areas in close proximity to their former homes. Three kinds of cases must be distinguished here: (1) the return of refugees to the places where they or their families originally lived and which are now built-up areas occupied by other people (for the most part, Jews) who live, work, and perform other activities there; (2) the return of refugees to vacant areas which are slotted for future construction, but are not the places from which these returnees originated; and (3) the return of refugees to areas which are not built-up at the moment but are earmarked for future development and which are also the places from which the potential returnees originated. With regard to the first category, liberals should have no difficulty in rejecting the Palestinian claim to return, at least if those now living in the places to which Palestinians are demanding to return are individuals who are not personally responsible for the fact that their lives have become rooted in these places nor for the injustice of the expulsion of the Palestinians in 1948. Regarding the second category—in which the return is not to the original places of Palestinian residence, which are now occupied, but rather to places

---

[10] Obviously, liberal nationalists could acknowledge that their liberal stances might be exploited and manipulated by nationalist movements such as Zionism, which create facts on the ground with normative significance which liberals are then forced to recognize. If these liberals are consequentialists, they could in principle recognize the legitimacy of supposedly nonliberal steps that might, in the long run, maximize the realization of liberalism. Problems of this kind also cast a shadow on such legal institutions as statutes of limitations. Yet I believe that these institutions are ultimately justified and more plausible from a liberal standpoint. For a convincing argument, see Waldron, "Settlement, Return and the Supersession Thesis."

which have not been settled by Israel and are earmarked for settlement in the future—the solution is more complex. Arguably, the response of liberal nationalists to this claim must be contingent upon what they consider to be the appropriate form of realizing the right to self-determination of the two nations residing in present-day Palestine/the Land of Israel. Those who espouse self-determination in the form of a single political framework for both nations that encompasses the whole area west of the Jordan River, in which the two nations are intertwined with no territorial separation between them, would doubtless argue that members of the Palestinian diaspora are entitled to return to areas currently within the borders of the State of Israel, just as they are entitled to settle in other parts of the area west of the Jordan River that are not currently within Israel's borders, since their original homeland comprises both of these areas, and their return to either of them would constitute a return to their homeland.

However, if liberal nationalists were to contend that Jewish and Palestinian self-determination should now be realized in separate territorial frameworks (either in two separate states or in one state with a clear territorial division between the two groups), then under such an arrangement, the place to which Palestinian refugees would return would first and foremost be contingent on how the territories of the Land of Israel west of the Jordan River were divided between the two nations. In terms of the liberal nationalist's position, rejecting the Zionist principle calling for the return of the Jews to the Land of Israel, Israel's pre-1967 borders are not sacrosanct, and neither are the borders determined by the 1947 UN Partition Plan, nor the borders determined by the new demographic reality created by the Jewish settlements in the occupied territories (the West Bank and the Gaza Strip) after the 1967 war. The issue of the appropriate borders to be adopted in the territorial separation solution to the Jewish-Palestinian dispute will be discussed in the next section of this chapter. In the present context, suffice it to say that, if territorial separation is the appropriate solution, then there are obvious advantages to a solution whereby Jewish responsibility for the Palestinian refugees is met by way of compensating the Palestinians for their suffering and by their repatriation exclusively to Palestinian territories. This is certainly the case regarding those unable to return to their families' original homes because these places are currently occupied by other individuals. If Palestinians could live in areas designated as Palestinian territories, this would be considered equivalent to living in their historic homeland at least to the same extent as living in territories designated for Jewish self-determination would be, since both potential places of residence belong to historic Palestine. However, since the Palestinians could express their culture more fully in exclusively Palestinian territories and since the Palestinian right to self-determination would primarily be realized there, collectivist considerations would favor a Palestinian return to these specific territories. These collectivist considerations would be decisive, in the light of the individualistic considerations militating against a Palestinian return to areas now inhabited by Jews who are not responsible for the fact that their lives are rooted there. Admittedly, it could be argued that Palestinian refugees whose former homes are currently inhabited by Jews might prefer living in geographic proximity to where their families originally lived, even within the areas of Jewish self-determination, as opposed to living in a territorial entity controlled by Palestinians, where they would enjoy national self-determination. However, most of the places in close physical proximity to the refugees' original homes have changed beyond recognition in terms of both their physical appearance and their social makeup.[11] Accordingly, even if proximity to their original homes is granted recognition as a factor to be considered in the final resolution of the conflict, it does not seem to be more important than living within their cultural group.

The considerations just mentioned are also germane to the third group of potential returnees, that is, those wishing to return to areas which at the moment are vacant but are earmarked for future construction and which are also the original homes of the potential returnees. The argument which invokes the fact that the lives of other individuals are currently established in these original places does not apply to members of this particular group. It could be argued that, at least in their case, Jewish responsibility for the injustice wrought by Zionism on the Palestinians should be realized by means of allowing their return to these places. This claim cannot be readily dismissed. And yet, even with regard to this group, it could reasonably be argued that, for many Palestinians, their places of origin can only be identified as such in the purely geographic sense, since the landscape and

---

[11] Palestinian refugees frequently visit old Palestinian buildings and the ruins of deserted villages, especially those that have not been replaced by Jewish settlements. They do so in search of traces of the way of life that once existed there, such as fragrant wildflowers that are used as spices. See Efrat Ben-Ze'ev, "The Politics of Taste and Smell: Palestinian Rites of Return," *Alpayim* 25 (2003), 73–88 (Hebrew). These visits may reflect a Palestinian interest in returning to these places. On the various interpretations of this interest, see Alon Harel, "Whose Home Is It? Reflections on the Palestinians' Interest in Return," *Theoretical Inquiries in Law* 5 (2004), 333–366.

character of these specific locations have changed beyond recognition. With regard to this group too, it could reasonably be argued that, since their culture would be expressed in a far more comprehensive sense in the Palestinian territories, and given that their right to self-determination would be primarily realized there, preference should be given to their repatriation in these areas. Furthermore, it could be argued that, notwithstanding the fact that the locations of their original homes are currently not built-up and are slotted for future construction, it might be more appropriate to designate these locations as building reserves for Jews and not for Arabs, since these particular places are within the territories designated for Jewish self-determination. It seems to me that balancing these considerations against the possibility of realizing Jewish responsibility for the travesties caused to Palestinians by means of allowing a return of Palestinian refugees would at most result in the return of a small number of Palestinians. I will return to this particular point immediately. However, it must first be recalled that the position advocated in this section—which rejects a mass Palestinian return and, at most, would allow the return of a limited number of Palestinian refugees—is ascribed to liberal nationalists who *deny* the justice of Zionism, since they believe that the principle of Jewish return to the Land of Israel was not valid at the particular time when the Zionist movement first embraced it. As stated above, if liberal nationalists who deny the justice of Zionism nonetheless object to a mass Palestinian return, then a fortiori, those who *affirm* the justice of the original Zionist aspiration for the Jews to return to the Land of Israel would also hold the position rejecting a mass return and accepting the return of a limited number of Palestinians. Liberal nationalists who reject Zionism and liberal nationalists who accept Zionist ideology might be divided over the question of responsibility and compensation, but not with regard to the question of Palestinian return.[12]

---

[12] Liberals who reject Zionism and liberals who accept Zionism might be divided over the question of responsibility and compensation, for if it was justified for the Jews to aspire to self-determination in the Land of Israel, then Zionism cannot be said to be exclusively responsible for Arab suffering. It can only be held responsible for the Palestinian suffering which resulted from the Zionist movement's attempts to achieve more than was justified. The extent to which Zionism is responsible for Palestinian suffering depends on the details of the justified version of Zionism and the gap between this version and what Zionism actually attempted. The answer to the question "Who else is responsible?" depends on the complex issues referred to in chapter 2 concerning the justification for the Jews' return to Palestine. These are issues of global distributive and remedial justice, as well as considerations regarding the defense of necessity in cases in which victims of people resorting to this defense are justified in resisting the trespassers.

The Return of a Limited Number of Palestinians and Zionist Responsibility for Palestinian Suffering

As has just been made clear, the most compelling argument against a Palestinian return—that the refugees' original homes and neighborhoods are currently inhabited by other individuals—does not apply in the case of those members of the Palestinian diaspora who originally came from areas which have not been settled by anyone else and which are earmarked for construction. Yet, there are two arguments against requiring the Jews to compensate these refugees for their suffering by allowing them to return to their original neighborhoods. First, the culture and the landscape of these places have changed completely. It is only in the geographical sense that they can be said to be the places where the refugees or their families originally lived.[13] Second, these places are located within territories mainly intended for the self-determination of the Jewish group. If these areas are land reserves for the future construction of residential areas, it is therefore appropriate that they be earmarked for members of the Jewish group. I do not dismiss these arguments out of hand. I merely wish to stress that they are not as strong as the arguments against return to original sites currently inhabited by other individuals.

In addition to the relative weakness of the arguments against the return of refugees to locations which are currently not occupied, it should be pointed out here that Israel's obligation to express its recognition of the special predicament which the Jews' return to Palestine created for the Palestinians, and the suffering which resulted from this predicament, could be invoked in support of the return of a small number of Palestinian refugees. If this is the case, then refugees from this group would be serious candidates for such a small-scale return of Palestinian refugees.

Israel's obligation to express recognition of the special predicament created by the Jews' return to Palestine ought to be acknowledged not only by those who reject Zionism because they deny the moral significance of the link between the Jewish people and the Land of Israel, but should also be recognized by those who accept Zionism. If my arguments in chapters 2 and 3 are sound, then Zionism could only be considered decisively and incontrovertibly just with the rise of fascism in Europe in the 1930s and especially in view of what later happened in the Holocaust. However, its incontrovertible justice was not the result of an Arab obligation to

---

[13] But see note 11 above, referring to the article by Ben-Ze'ev.

compensate the Jews for persecution, since they were not responsible for persecution of the Jews in Europe. Zionism became unequivocally justified at that time because of the convergence of the urgent necessity for Jewish self-determination due to the persecution suffered by the Jews with the general principle of global distributive justice, according to which it is appropriate for nations to select the site of their self-determination in territories with which they have a formative link. I have argued that this principle is only one of a whole set of still-unspecified principles determining criteria for settling issues such as the territorial scope of self-determination, its appropriate institutional form, and so on, which together comprise an ideal theory of global justice. This particular principle applies to one detail pertaining to the allocation of the world's territories among nations in a manner that would allow them to realize their right to self-determination. In a world that has no recognized institutions qualified or empowered to formulate the entire complex of relevant principles at the level of specificity required for their implementation and for enforcing these principles, applying this principle to only one case might cause a great deal of injustice, even if it concurrently also brings about justice.[14] However, even though applying this principle of global justice to merely one case could be considered problematic, it was justified in the Jewish case because of the necessity created by the rise of fascism and the Holocaust. Nonetheless, the claim that it caused considerable injustice to the Arabs is still a valid one. The Arabs were the only ones required to pay the price of the Jews' return. If the appropriate institutions for the implementation of international justice had existed, the responsibility for the Jewish predicament at the time could perhaps have been evenly divided among all of the nations, especially among those nations that had been directly responsible for creating the immediate necessity for Jewish political self-determination. As I argued in chapter 2, this is why Arab resistance toward Zionism is understandable and even justified. Even those who maintain that the specific circumstances of the 1930s and 1940s rendered Zionism incontrovertibly justified must acknowledge this.[15]

A second and perhaps more important reason that Israel ought to recognize at least partial responsibility for the wrongs experienced by the Palestinians is that Zionism has in fact gone beyond the limits justified even by

---

[14] For a detailed discussion, see chapter 2, section 3.

[15] See chapter 2, section 4.

the circumstances created in the aftermath of the Holocaust. In other words, although it may have been justified for the Jewish people to aspire to establish a state in the Land of Israel, and even though this aspiration became absolutely just in the 1930s and 1940s, it was certainly not just to aspire to do so within the borders created in 1948. Even if the war that the Jewish state fought for its independence was forced upon it, thereby becoming a just war, this did not justify expulsions, nor did it justify the confiscation of land and houses that had been left by those who fled in fear of the war.[16] Admittedly, some of these actions may merit forgiveness because of the exceptional circumstances of the times and the justifiable fears engendered by those circumstances (namely, heightened Jewish fears due to what the Jews had experienced in the Holocaust and in view of the strident Arab rejection of the UN resolution which called for the establishment of a Jewish state). Nevertheless, not all of the Jewish community's actions can be considered justified. Israel therefore should acknowledge a certain degree of responsibility for the injustices experienced by the Palestinians. Granting a limited number of Palestinian refugees the possibility of returning to the places within the borders of the Jewish state from which their families originated could be one significant way of expressing this recognition.[17] However, this is not the only way to do so, and I am not convinced that it is the best way to express this recognition. I will return to this matter in the next section of the chapter in my discussion of the appropriate division of the territories west of the Jordan River.

2. THE ISSUE OF TERRITORIAL DIVISION AND THE 1967 BORDERS

The June 5, 1967, Borders

Above, my objection to a mass return of Palestinian refugees to the Jewish state was not because Zionism is not responsible for the demographic upheavals it created, but because such a return is not the appropriate way

---

[16] In this regard, see Andrei Marmor, "Entitlement to Land and the Right of Return: An Embarrassing Challenge for Liberal Zionism," in Lukas H. Meyer (ed.), *Justice in Time: Responding to Historical Injustice* (Baden-Baden: Nomos, 2004), 319–333.

[17] For the view that it is necessary to recognize this Israeli responsibility, but also that the means for fulfilling this responsibility need not be mass return, see Harel, "Whose Home Is It?" especially 341–343.

to realize this responsibility. However, if Zionism is indeed responsible for rectifying the demographic situation that resulted from the realization of Zionist aspirations, then it must also be held responsible for rectifying the state of affairs that resulted from how the territories were ultimately divided between the two nations. Andrei Marmor explained why this territorial division is problematic. He noted that, if one purchases a piece of land and other people trespass on it, conceivably one is then entitled to use violent measures to remove the trespassers. However, their act of trespassing does not entitle the landowner to seize additional land.[18] In other words, even if the Jews were justified in repelling the Arab armies that threatened to forcibly revoke the UN resolution of November 29, 1947, which was intended to establish two states within the borders specified in that resolution, this did not justify their view that all of the territories conquered in 1948 were territories in which they were entitled to realize Jewish self-determination. Accordingly, if one accepts the position that Palestinian refugees who cannot return to their places of origin should not be repatriated to vacant areas in the Jewish state, this does not entail that they should not be allowed to return to vacant areas that are *currently* within the borders of the State of Israel. Conceivably, they could be allowed to return to such areas, which would then cease to be Israeli and become Palestinian. But is this an appropriate solution?

As noted earlier, an overwhelming majority of Israelis, including those belonging to the Zionist Left, reject such a solution. The borders of the Jewish state determined in the ceasefire at the end of the 1948 Israeli War of Independence are sacred to them, at least *as the basis* for the division of the western part of the Land of Israel. On the one hand, they oppose withdrawal from these borders to the narrower borders of the partition plan under the UN resolution of November 29, 1947. On the other hand, at least the Zionist Left opposes expanding these borders to include Jewish settlements established in the territories conquered in the 1967 war, unless the Palestinian state is given equivalent territorial compensation. I believe this position to be appropriate at least as a general rule, because the pre-1967 borders were internationally recognized and could therefore undergird a peace treaty between Israel and a Palestinian state. Indeed, borders beyond those of 1967 have never been accorded international recognition, and under the current conditions, it is unlikely that such recognition will ever

---

[18] Marmor, "Entitlement to Land and the Right of Return," 321.

be granted. Moreover, those borders forestall any possibility of an agree-ment between the Jews and Palestinians that would provide the Palestinians with a modicum of self-respect. Acceptable borders must demonstrate at least some consideration for Palestinian suffering and losses in the past and facilitate an independent and respectful existence in the future.

Of course, it could be argued that, while these are valid reasons for preferring the pre-1967 borders over expanded borders, they do not jus-tify preferring the pre-1967 borders over narrower borders. Obviously, nar-rower borders could similarly accommodate the possibility of peace between the Jews and Palestinians. It would almost certainly enhance its prospects, and there is no reason to assume that such borders would not enjoy international recognition. But this argument overlooks the reason for viewing the inter-national recognition enjoyed by the pre-1967 borders as sufficient grounds for accepting them as the appropriate borders between the Jews and Arabs in Palestine. It is not that these borders are inherently just. Rather, there is no clear answer to the question of what would constitute a just territorial division between the Arabs and Jews specifically or among national groups in general. In drawing the territorial boundaries of national entities for the purpose of self-determination, complex moral considerations of distribu-tive justice come into play. These pertain to the size of the national groups, the nature of their cultures, and the collective and individual needs of their members. The needs of other national groups in the world and the scarcity of global territorial resources must also be taken into consideration.

Clearly, widespread agreement on comprehensive moral solutions to these problems (even if, in principle, such solutions might exist) is virtually impossible due to the limitations of human nature. This is certainly the case in the Jewish-Palestinian dispute. When determining the appropriate size of the Palestinian state compared to the size of the Jewish state, the only points that should not be in dispute are the following presumptions: First, any mass transfers of population groups are unacceptable. Second, any state to be formed should be of a feasible size. Third, the territory of any given state should be continuous land and not consist of unconnected bits and pieces. However, even these seemingly indisputable issues are open to equivocation and debate. For example, what constitutes "mass" population transfer? Are there any conditions that override any of the above presumptions? Other considerations that factor into the territorial division process are even more controversial. For example, should the territorial borders of the Jewish state be based solely on the size of the current Jewish population in Israel or should the fact that Israel perceives itself as the home for all Jews be taken into account and the borders determined in anticipation of their possible immigration in the future? Should the territorial borders of the Palestinian state be determined in light of the possibility that all members of the Palestinian diaspora may ultimately settle there? Should consideration be given to the fact that such a state enjoys significant political and cultural affinity with the Arab states? How much unpopulated space is necessary to accommodate the recreational needs of the populations of each of the two states?

Conceivably, there are clear and precise answers to these questions. Yet, in reality, there are differences of opinion within each of the parties to the Jewish-Palestinian conflict, and certainly between the Jews and the Palestinians, as to how to answer them. This situation of moral ambiguities and disagreements makes it imperative for the disputing parties to reach a compromise. Israel's pre-1967 borders provide a firm foundation for such a compromise by virtue of the international community's recognition of these borders. Any attempt to reach a compromise based on any other borders, whether narrower or wider, would lead to further disputes which would not easily be resolved. Moreover, since it is morally incumbent on both sides to prevent the perpetuation of violence, any attempt to formulate a compromise based on anything but the pre-1967 borders must be rejected, as this would only lead to a stalemate between the two sides and to further violence. In other words, the pre-1967 borders constitute the best lines along which the Palestinians and Jews should be separated not because these borders are inherently more just than any other option within the infinite range of reasonable possibilities for just borders, but because it is difficult to come up with any conclusive reason for preferring any of the other options. The clear advantage of the pre-1967 borders is the international recognition they already enjoy.[19] The fact that international recognition for any other borders might be secured *after* a territorial agreement has been reached between the parties does not provide the parties with means for deciding what those borders should be *before* they have reached

---

[19]   However, it is important to remind supporters of this position (namely, the Israeli Left) of two additional positions taken by the international community. One asserts Israel's duty to allow the return of at least a certain number of Palestinian refugees (UN General Assembly Resolution 194 [III]) and the other is the international community's refusal to recognize Jerusalem as the capital of Israel. Invoking international recognition of the pre-1967 borders as the grounds for making them the borders between the Palestinian and the Jewish states entails taking the other two positions, which also relate to the very heart of the Arab-Israeli conflict, into consideration.

an agreement. In other words, the existing international recognition of the pre-1967 borders provides moral grounds for favoring these borders not only because this recognition is indeed *international* but also, and perhaps primarily, because this recognition *already exists*. It constitutes an anchor for the resolution of a moral dispute the ending of which constitutes an urgent moral imperative, while there is a slim chance of finding any solution other than territorial separation on the basis of these borders.[20]

From the moral viewpoint, the territorial division of Palestine/the Land of Israel between a state in which Palestinians enjoy self-determination and one in which self-determination is enjoyed primarily by the Jews should therefore be based on the pre-1967 borders. Regarding the Palestinian claim for the return of the 1948 refugees, this position means a rejection of the mass return of refugees not only to places within the borders of the Jewish state but to all of the places where these refugees originally came from, since these are all within the pre-1967 borders of Israel.

However, the above only applies to a *mass* return of Palestinian refugees. In the previous section, I argued that there are good reasons for the Jewish state to allow a limited Palestinian return, mainly of those refugees whose original lands are currently unoccupied by others. These reasons pertain to the duty incumbent on the Jewish state to express its recognition of the special predicament which the Jews' return to Palestine created for the Palestinians, and the suffering which resulted from this predicament. These are

---

[20] Moral problems which seem to have several possible solutions, none of which can clearly be said to be superior to any of the other options, are similar to coordination problems. Ordinary coordination problems are those in which the parties have an interest in cooperating with one another. In order to cooperate with one another, the parties in question could agree on one of several different options, none of which is necessarily superior to the other. The problem, therefore, is which one should be chosen. In our context, the problems are not of a kind that the parties are necessarily interested in solving. However, they have a moral obligation to solve them. There are many reasonable moral solutions to the matter of the territorial division between the Jews and Arabs in the area west of the Jordan River. International recognition of a particular territorial division could help to determine which solution should be chosen. Obviously, there could be other ways of reaching the decision, such as tossing a coin between reasonable territorial divisions. However, even within the scope of reasonable territorial divisions, the possibilities are endless and the parties could take forever just trying to decide between which of these possibilities they should toss a coin. For example, let us assume that the alternatives for a reasonable solution are somewhere between the British Royal Commission's 1937 partition plan and the borders that Ariel Sharon was supposed to propose as part of the "Roadmap" process initiated by President George W. Bush in 2002. Even within this framework, there are an infinite number of possibilities, because one can forever add or remove variations that differ only fractionally from any other option for borders.

good reasons not only for a return of a small number of Palestinians whose original lands are currently unoccupied by other individuals within the borders of the Jewish state, but also for simultaneously giving these areas to the Palestinian state.[21] In view of my arguments for rejecting the Palestinian return to the Jewish state, which derive from the justification for dividing Palestine into two states, there are clear advantages to allowing a return of a small number of refugees to the places from which they originally came while the Jews also cede such areas to the Palestinian state. One advantage is that it expresses recognition not only of the demographic injustice caused to the Palestinians in 1948, but also of the territorial injustice inflicted on them then. A second advantage is that it serves the interests of the returnees not only in returning to the places from which they originated but also in living in these places in the framework of a state in which their group exercises its right to self-determination. A third advantage is that it does not further aggravate the anxieties of Israel with regard to its future demographic makeup and helps to preserve its character as the Jewish state.

The 1948 Evils, the Evils following 1967, and Moral Consistency

The argument most commonly invoked in Israeli public debates for rejecting the concept of the return of Palestinian refugees is the Jewish character of Israel. Almost universally accepted by the Israeli public, this argument is also invoked by the Zionist Left. Challenging this argument, Andrei Marmor claimed that, if ethnic cleansing is a legitimate means of securing the cultural character of states, then why not secure this character by placing restrictions on the political and civil rights of minorities (or even the majority)?[22] Marmor implied that the Zionist Left does not have too many choices: It must either abandon its opposition to the return of Palestinian refugees or else admit that it is not truly liberal. Furthermore, in Marmor's view, from a

---

[21] An example for the present purpose is certain areas east of Beit Govrin. These are areas which are not densely populated by Jews and are remote from concentrations of Jewish population, and they are close to areas populated by Arabs east of the pre-1967 borders. The areas in question are currently used as training grounds by the army, and there are no long-term Israeli plans for this particular territory. These areas are also not in that part of pre-1967 Israel which is extremely narrow. If the Jewish state gives up an area of around 20 square kilometers in this region, tens of thousands of refugees could return to live there, and it would then be possible to allocate it to the Palestinian state. In this context, it is worth mentioning that, in the peace treaty with Jordan, Israel gave up an area of 300 square kilometers in the Arava region in the south of Israel. (My thanks to Arnon Golan for the information included in this note.)

[22] Marmor, "Entitlement to Land and the Right of Return," 331–332.

moral perspective, Israel's borders prior to June 4, 1967, are no more defensible than the (expanded) borders that include post-1967 settlements in the occupied territories. In both cases, the borders were the result of a war; and war, however justified a particular war might be, is not a legitimate means for territorial acquisition. Paradoxically, the Israeli Right also makes the same argument. However, it does so in order to arrive at the opposite conclusion, presumably by invoking the historical rights argument. In an interview published in the newspaper *Yedioth Ahronoth*, the late Yosef Ben-Shlomo, a professor of philosophy and a resident of Kedumim, a Jewish settlement in Samaria, stated, "[Describing] Judea and Samaria as 'occupied territories' is both intellectual and linguistic prostitution."[23] He further noted:

> Katamon [a neighborhood within the pre-1967 Jerusalem municipality] is occupied territory, and the houses in which the leaders of Peace Now currently live are occupied territory, and Sheikh Munis [an Arab village which was situated on the site where Tel Aviv University is located today], where all the left-wing professors reside and attack me, is an Arab village whose residents were expelled. So how do these areas differ from Kedumim [a post-1967 settlement].[24]

These accusations of inconsistency are unfounded. I will begin with the claim according to which the desire to maintain the Jewish character of Israel does not justify a rejection of the return of Palestinian refugees, which would mean the perpetuation of the results of ethnic cleansing, any more than it justifies imposing restrictions on the civil and political rights of the Arab citizens of Israel. There are a number of possible responses to this claim. First, from the viewpoint of those considering how to make up for it now, one could point out that the expulsion of Palestinians from certain areas in Palestine cannot be said to have been a planned policy designed for the future but, rather, an exceptional, local event that occurred almost 60 years ago and that requires a response now, in the current state of affairs.[25]

---

[23] Quoted in Amira Lam, "Let It Be Bad," *Yedioth Ahronoth: Seven Days* weekend magazine (December 6, 2002), 28 (Hebrew).

[24] Ibid.

[25] One could claim that each and every day that the refugees are not allowed to return to their original homes is morally tantamount to re-expelling them. This view is perhaps plausible only from the victims' viewpoint. It cannot be acceptable from the perspective of those who have to decide what to do with the victims by balancing their suffering with other considerations, such as the potential suffering of those who now happen to be living in the places from which the Palestinians were once expelled. The accusation of daily ethnic cleansing is therefore unreasonable.

Preventing the perpetuation of the suffering it caused and is still causing does not require the repatriation of all of the victims. On the other hand, deliberately restricting the political rights of Israeli Arabs so as to preserve the Jewish character of the state constitutes a permanent arrangement, the consequences of which cannot be mitigated by anything less than its total abandonment.

Furthermore, compensation for the suffering that resulted from the 1948 expulsion of the Palestinians may indeed be imperative, but the means for rectifying this wrong should also reflect other aspects of a complex moral predicament. For example, the Jews in Israel harbor well-founded security concerns regarding the presence of a large indigenous population in their midst who reject the establishment of the State of Israel and who experienced great losses and injustice as a result. Quite naturally, it is unlikely for any latent hostility to be immediately placated by any Israeli actions intended to atone for these wrongs.

It could also be pointed out that there are moral differences among various cases in which ethnic groups were expelled from where they lived. For example, the Serbs' ethnic purge of the Muslims in Bosnia at the beginning of the 1990s did not resemble the expulsion of the Sudetenland Germans by the Czechs in the aftermath of World War II. Even if one does not justify the expulsion of the Palestinians in 1948, the particular circumstances under which it was committed may constitute grounds for excusing it, provided that the Jews acknowledge their responsibility for the wrongs committed and offer compensation by means other than allowing the actual return of refugees.

The second accusation of inconsistency that requires a response is that the pre-1967 borders are no more morally justifiable than the borders that include settlements created after 1967, since both are, on the one hand, within the area of the historic Land of Israel and, on the other hand, the product of wars. Even if these wars might have been just, they cannot justify territorial acquisition. Ben-Shlomo on the Right and Marmor on the Left both noted that the only borders of Israel which are internationally recognized are the borders that were adopted by the November 29, 1947, UN resolution on the partition of Palestine.[26] They both argued that the expulsion of the inhabitants of Sheikh Munis perpetrated a greater moral injustice than the settlement of Kedumim, because the latter was

---

[26] Lam, "Let It Be Bad," 28; Marmor, "Entitlement to Land and the Right of Return," 324.

established on land from which no one was expelled. Anyone trying to argue otherwise is "prostituting the intellect," in Ben-Shlomo's words, or is prepared to adopt inconsistent positions, according to Marmor.[27] For Ben-Shlomo, consistency combined with his right-wing value judgments require that Israel adopt policies enabling it to take control of the entire Land of Israel by the force of the Jews' historical rights to the Land of Israel. One way or another, this necessitates the commission of acts that are patently unjust. According to Ben-Shlomo, however, it seems that such acts would be justified by the supreme moral importance of the historical right of the Jewish people to the Land of Israel. According to him, anyone rejecting this position and relying exclusively on international legitimacy as the basis for Israel's borders must, for consistency's sake, support withdrawal to the 1947 partition borders. Marmor's left-wing position leads to the same conclusion.

In my opinion, however, both Ben-Shlomo and Marmor are wrong. With regard to the requirements of consistency pertaining to the historical rights argument, the claim according to which support for Jewish presence in Tel Aviv necessarily entails support for Jewish presence in Nablus is fallacious, even if historical rights are interpreted as providing a justification for the right to territorial sovereignty. Even if historical rights justify Jewish sovereignty both over Tel Aviv and over Nablus, other moral and pragmatic considerations could justify compromising the realization of these rights. The willingness to compromise does not always imply inconsistency.[28] However, if my arguments in chapter 2 are correct, and historical rights are interpreted as they ought to be interpreted, namely, not as a basis for the actual right to territorial sovereignty, but rather as a basis for deciding on

[27] Lam, "Let It Be Bad," 28; Marmor, "Entitlement to Land and the Right of Return."

[28] It is doubtful whether this should even be conceived of as a compromise. People subscribing to the view that historical rights justify Jewish sovereignty over all of the Land of Israel could for either similar or different reasons also maintain that the Palestinians and the Jordanians have the right to sovereignty over these areas. This would then result in a conflict of rights that would have to be resolved one way or another (by dividing the sovereignty over the area or by dividing the area), just as all conflicts between moral and practical considerations must be resolved. Even people who argue that the considerations supporting Arab rights to the land cannot compete with the Jews' historical rights and that only the latter could be a basis for sovereignty could, without risking inconsistency, waive realization of the Jewish historical right for pragmatic reasons that carry moral force. For example, some supporters of the 1937 Peel Plan thought it should be accepted because of the need to rescue the Jews of Europe. They believed that a sovereign state would help this urgent need even if it did not cover the whole of the Land of Israel.

the geographical site for national self-determination, then there is surely no inconsistency in a willingness to determine the site for the realization of Jewish self-determination in only part of the Land of Israel rather than in the entire territory. On the contrary, if historical rights merely serve as a consideration that justifies selecting the site of national self-determination *within* territories located in a historic homeland, and not as a consideration that fully justifies the right to territorial sovereignty, let alone in *all* of the territories of the historic homeland, then it is precisely those who invoke historical rights in order to claim territorial sovereignty over the entire historic homeland who are inconsistent. Unlike cases such as Bismarck's demand for German sovereignty over Alsace-Lorraine in the wake of the Prussian-French War in 1870, or Masaryk's demand for the Sudetenland at the end of World War I, or Saddam Hussein's claim to Kuwait after invading it in 1991, there is no need whatsoever to interpret the historical rights argument invoked by Zionism before the establishment of the State of Israel as a basis for territorial sovereignty and territorial expansion. Indeed, there is a tremendous difference between the historical rights argument as used in the early days of Zionism and the way this argument is currently used by the messianic Gush Emunim settlers' movement and people like Ben-Shlomo. The earlier use of the historical rights argument could be interpreted as invoking these rights for the sake of merely selecting the site for Jewish self-determination. Zionism's current reliance on historical rights can only be interpreted as invoking these rights for the sake of justifying the territorial expansion of a people which already enjoys self-determination.

With regard to the consistency required by the international legitimacy argument, the claim that this commits one to support withdrawal to the 1947 partition borders is problematic because it takes for granted that the 1947 partition plan is the appropriate source of international legitimacy with regard to Israel's borders. However, this is not necessarily the case. The partition plan could be regarded as having established morally legitimate borders for the Jewish state for two different reasons. One reason is that it was an international solution to a problem lacking any other clear moral solution, and given the plan's potential for the prevention of continued violence, it was incumbent upon the parties to the Israeli-Palestinian conflict to adopt this solution. Alternatively, given the relevant parameters at the time, the 1947 UN Partition Plan could be regarded as having come up with the morally appropriate solution, since it separated the areas with a Jewish majority from those areas that had an Arab majority. However, neither of these considerations was still valid in the period immediately preceding the

Six-Day War in June 1967 and immediately after the war. In 1947, the partition plan was both a reasonable and internationally recognized solution to a
problem which had no other clear solution. This was not the case in 1967.
In 1967, Israel enjoyed international recognition within the borders that
had been determined by the 1949 ceasefire lines at the end of Israel's 1948
War of Independence. This recognition replaced the international recognition provided by the UN Partition Plan of 1947.[29] Accordingly, Marmor's
argument concerning the international recognition of the 1947 borders can
no longer be presented as an argument for a return to those borders.

Let us now turn to the argument that the 1947 partition plan ought
to have been adopted because it separated the areas with a Jewish majority
from those areas that had an Arab majority. Clearly, since the demographic
reality in Palestine/the Land of Israel in 1967 was very different from the
demographic situation in 1947, a different territorial division was called for
in 1967. Of course, since there are areas within the 1967 borders which were
then and still are unpopulated, such a division would not necessarily have
to go along with the pre-Six-Day-War borders. In fact, narrower borders
might conceivably be appropriate. However, for demographic reasons, the
borders can no longer be adjusted to conform to the partition plan lines of
1947. From the perspective of 2006, the year this chapter was written, borders that extend beyond those before the 1967 war might well be required.
In any case, there is no clear moral criterion for determining whether the
borders should today be narrower or wider than the pre-1967 borders, for
international consensus only exists with respect to the pre-1967 borders. It
therefore makes a lot of sense to claim that these should be the recognized
borders, or at least the basis for such borders.

Not only do Marmor and Ben-Shlomo ignore and belittle these considerations, they also claim that borders beyond the pre-1967 borders would
be more legitimate than the post-1949/pre-1967 borders, since the former
would be drawn in accordance with settlements on lands not acquired by
way of ethnic cleansing, whereas the latter were based on borders that were

---

[29] On this matter, it is important to note the advisory opinion of the International Court of
Justice dated July 9, 2004, on the construction of the Israeli separation wall in the Palestinian territories. See International Court of Justice, Legal Consequences of the Construction of the Wall in
the Occupied Palestinian Territory, Advisory Opinion (July 9, 2004). This opinion is the first to
manifest *legal* recognition of the pre-1967 borders (see paragraph 67 and elsewhere in the decision). It should, however, be noted that this legal recognition is based on previous international
political recognition. (I am grateful to Eyal Benvenisti for bringing this to my attention.)

largely the consequence of ethnic cleansing. Marmor therefore argues that, if it is at all possible to compare the moral worth of the borders determined after Israel's 1948 War of Independence to those created by the settlements established after 1967, then the latter must be considered morally superior. He believes that the only reasons for compromising on the post-1967 borders are pragmatic rather than principled. Despite his admission that these pragmatic reasons also have a moral dimension, since the motivation to act on them derives from the moral imperative to resolve conflicts, Marmor's description of these reasons as pragmatic in effect underplays the significance of this moral imperative.

Is Marmor's argumentation sound? Admittedly, seizure of lands by way of ethnic cleansing is, other things being equal, graver than attaining them in a manner not involving that crime. However, there are strong reasons for arguing that the ethnic cleansing that took place in 1948 was less morally reprehensible than the ongoing settlement activity subsequent to the 1967 Six-Day War. First, the ethnic cleansing of 1948, even if it was deliberately perpetrated by part or all of the Jewish political leadership in the Land of Israel, is attributable to the Jews' heightened fears due to their experiences in World War II and the understandable urgency with which they sought to establish a state that would provide them with protection. The Arabs opposed the establishment of such a state. Even though this claim is part of the Zionist narrative, I believe that it is true. In contrast, the settlements following the 1967 war were on behalf of, or at least under the aegis of, an existing state. They were established for the purpose of territorial expansion under circumstances that provided no basis for the fears that may have been justified in 1948. Second, if my arguments concerning the appropriateness of the 1967 borders are sound, then the Israeli governments and other political agents who initiated the settlements should have known that the post-1967 settlements would create almost insurmountable obstacles on the road to peace and the resolution of the violent conflict with the Arabs. The moral duty to refrain from creating such obstacles is, in my view, no less of a moral duty than the duty not to undermine the partition plan of 1947. Taking steps to prevent any possibility of complying with this moral duty, which has characterized the circumstances and policies of the settlement project, prepares the ground for future ethnic cleansings, which would be absolutely unpardonable.

I therefore return to the position that I defended above regarding the main aspects of the demographic distribution of Jews and Arabs and the division of the territory west of the Jordan River. Accordingly, the territorial division should be based on the pre-1967 borders and Jewish recognition of responsibility for the wrongs inflicted by the Zionist movement on the Palestinians. As a rule, the concrete realization of Jewish responsibility should not be by way of the mass return of refugees to the places from which they originated within the Jewish state, nor to their original locations in general. I proposed considering an exception to this rule mainly because of the need to express Jewish recognition of the high price paid by the Palestinians for the realization of both the justified and unjustified aspects of Zionism. The Jewish state could demonstrate this recognition either by allowing the return of a small and clearly defined number of Palestinians to the sites of their original homes within the State of Israel, or by allowing the return of a small and clearly defined number of Palestinians to their places of origin and simultaneously relinquishing these particular areas to the Palestinian state. I argued that the latter is preferable mainly because it allows Israel to demonstrate its recognition of the Jewish responsibility for Palestinian suffering without undermining the demographic rationale for the division of Palestine into two states. One state would constitute the realization of Jewish self-determination, while the other would be the manifestation of Palestinian self-determination.

Palestinians in the Jewish State, Jews in the Palestinian State, and the Exchange of Territories

Some political parties and politicians in Israel have suggested the idea of transferring areas located within the pre-1967 borders and settled by Palestinians who are Israeli citizens to the territorial boundaries of the state designated for Palestinian self-determination.[30] The emphasis in the proposed border change is not on the return of Palestinian refugees to their former homes but rather on transferring Israeli areas bordering on the pre-1967 borders and populated by Palestinian citizens of Israel who did not flee from their homes in 1948 into the Palestinian state. This suggestion is sometimes made by politicians as one part of an agreement that would include an exchange of territories. The complementary component of such an exchange would be that areas beyond Israel's pre-1967 borders where Jewish settlements have been established would be designated as belonging

---

[30] For example, it is an important part of the platform presented by the Israel Beytenu Party in the 2006 Knesset elections. The same idea had previously been suggested by Member of Knesset Ephraim Sneh of the Labor Party.

to the State of Israel. However, what motivates those supporting the idea of allocating pre-1967 Israeli territories populated by Israeli Palestinians to the Palestinian state is not that they wish to reciprocate the annexation of Jewish settlements to Israel but rather that such a status change would serve to change the ratio of Jews to Arabs in Israel by decreasing the number of Arabs living within the State of Israel. Clearly, this suggestion comports with the logic of the division of the territories west of the Jordan River into two separate ethnocultural states. In chapter 3, I supported this division due to the history of the Jewish-Palestinian conflict. This division might be supported by others not only for this reason but also because they generally prefer to live in political units that have as much ethnocultural homogeneity as possible.

However, it is important to note that the transfer of areas within the pre-1967 borders of Israel populated by Israeli Palestinians to the Palestinian state is considerably more problematic morally than the transfer to the Palestinian state of areas within Israel's pre-1967 borders to which Palestinian refugees are slotted to return. The latter case is not one in which residents of a given area are required to replace a way of life to which they are interested in adhering and perhaps even important components of identity that they have acquired in the course of a significant portion of their lives. Palestinian refugees returning to their places of origin which have been transferred to the Palestinian state would not be required to change their lives for the worse nor to relinquish part of their identities. Nor would they suffer a decline in their standard of living; quite the contrary is more likely. On the other hand, Palestinian citizens of Israel, who have grown up in Israel and live in areas intended to be handed over to the Palestinian state, will lose on all of these fronts. Growing up in Israel has accustomed them to economic, social, cultural, and political conditions which in many respects may be considered by many of them (and by reasonable people in general) as superior to the lives they are likely to have in the future Palestinian state. For some of them, the economic, social, and political characteristics of life in Israel have become part of their identities. For all of these reasons, the possibility of transferring areas bordering on the pre-1967 lines and settled by Palestinian citizens of Israel into the borders of the Palestinian state should not depend exclusively on the consent of the parties to the Jewish-Palestinian conflict, that is, the Jews living west of the Jordan River and the official representatives of the Palestinian people. It would also require the consent of the particular Palestinian residents of the areas which are currently part of Israel and which are slotted for the Palestinian state.

Irrespective of whether or not some of them agree to such an arrangement, Palestinians will clearly continue to be a significant minority in the Jewish state because a considerable number of Israel's Palestinian citizens do not live in proximity to the pre-1967 borders, and the areas in which they live are not potentially transferable in the manner discussed above. This means that self-determination in the framework of the Israeli pre-1967 borders cannot be exclusively for Jews. Certain Israeli politicians and public figures believe that, by the same token, self-determination in the future Palestinian state should also not be exclusively for Palestinians. They believe that some of the Jewish settlements established after 1967 should remain within the areas of the Palestinian state, even if settlements that border on the pre-1967 lines should be annexed to the Jewish state (and even if other settlements should be evacuated, as in the case of the evacuation of the settlements on the Gaza Strip in 2005). This proposal is motivated by a desire for symmetry in two respects: (a) the degree of ethnic homogeneity in each of the two states, and (b) the way the two ethnocultural groups might benefit from the presence of their respective groups in all of the areas perceived by them as their historic homeland, even if neither of them has cultural and political dominance in the whole of this historic homeland. Given the importance ascribed by ethnocultural nationalism to the connection between national groups and their historic homelands (see chapter 2), it is difficult to deny the force of this second reason for leaving Israeli settlements in the Palestinian areas. Moreover, in chapter 3, by invoking the value of pluralism, I argued against the desirability of interpreting the right to ethnocultural self-determination as entailing the particular ethnocultural group's right to exclusive presence in the territory in which it realizes its right to self-determination. Pluralism could be used to justify allowing some of the Jewish settlements in the Palestinian areas to remain there, since ethnic diversity would conceivably benefit Palestinian society. And yet, it is important to emphasize that these reasons for leaving the Jewish settlements in the Palestinian areas, though they may be powerful, should not necessarily figure most prominently in any final decisions.

In 1993, immediately after the Oslo Accords, the writer A. B. Yehoshua and other prominent Israeli intellectuals published a petition in support of leaving some of the Jewish settlements within the borders of the Palestinian state.[31] They justified this demand by giving reasons similar to those

---

[31] See A. B. Yehoshua, "The Third Way," *Ha'aretz* (November 19, 1993), B5 (Hebrew).

mentioned above. The petition encountered considerable resistance in both left- and right-wing circles. The left-wing opposition claimed that the settlement movement was trying to undermine the peace process. It also reminded the Israeli public of facts concerning the unruly nature of many of the settlers. The right-wing opponents of this petition argued that the intentions of at least certain Palestinian groups regarding such an arrangement could not truly be peaceful, and that consequently, leaving settlers under Palestinian rule would in effect mean abandoning them. Both of these objections seem to override the principled reasons for leaving some of the Israeli settlers in Palestinian areas. Yehoshua was quick to respond that his suggestion to leave the settlers within the borders of the Palestinian state was only intended for those settlers who would agree to remain and who would further commit themselves to living peacefully alongside their Palestinian neighbors without any provocative acts or violence. Furthermore, he claimed that his proposal was intended to be within the framework of an agreement with the Palestinian state that would also include the Palestinian state's commitment to provide security for these settlements.[32] If I believed that such a promise could indeed be trusted, then I could perhaps accept Yehoshua's response. However, in view of contemporary events, I am not convinced that this is the case. Putting aside these pragmatic considerations, I wish to stress that the principled positions for which I have argued throughout this book support the possibility of leaving some or all of the Jewish settlements in a future Palestinian state.

The final terms of the division of the land west of the Jordan River into two states may prescribe that areas occupied by a significant part of the Palestinian citizens of Israel should become part of the Palestinian state or, alternatively, remain part of the Jewish state. In these final arrangements, Jewish settlements could either be left within the borders of the Palestinian state or be completely evacuated. However, in reality, the division into two states is unlikely to be completely symmetrical. In one of the states, the beneficiaries of self-determination will be mainly the Jews, but the many indigenous Palestinians should also be entitled to certain group rights (for example, autonomy in education and various representation rights). I will discuss this in greater detail in the next chapter. The other state should be the main place where Palestinian self-determination is realized, though Palestinians would also have certain cultural and political group rights in the

---

[32]   See A. B. Yehoshua, "The Third Way," *Ha'aretz* (November 19, 1993), B5 (Hebrew).

country that is mainly Jewish. The question of whether Jews would benefit from such rights within the Palestinian state depends on whether or not some of the Israeli settlements can be left there. Although, as I just noted, this is in principle worthy of support, it is probably not feasible in practice. These conclusions commonly arouse resentment in Israel and are popularly expressed in the grievance that the Palestinians would get "a state and a half" while the Jews would have to do with just "half a state."[33]

In response to this, a number of facts must be mentioned which may assuage this protest and reveal its self-righteous nature. First of all, a large Arab community has lived within the pre-1967 borders of Israel for generations and is therefore a native community entitled to some collective rights. The same would apply to Jews in the Palestinian state, if some of the Jewish settlements remain within its borders. If no such settlements remain, this would be the result of an agreement between the Jewish and Palestinian states. Second, the division of the territories west of the Jordan River into two states on the basis of the pre-1967 borders allocates almost four-fifths of this territory to the Jews, whereas the Palestinians, who until the end of the nineteenth century were almost the sole residents of this territory, get only one-fifth of the area. Third, even assuming that the Jews would not be the sole beneficiaries of rights of cultural preservation and self-rule within the Jewish state—as opposed to the Palestinians' exclusive rights within the Palestinian state—they would still enjoy limited hegemony protected by a number of arrangements. They would not only enjoy the ordinary privileges to which every ethnocultural nation is entitled in its homeland (for example, language privileges, priorities in immigration, etc.), but would also have special privileges which the Palestinians living in Israel—a homeland group—would not have. The privileges in question would provide them with demographic hegemony and control over security issues, insofar as this is required for security reasons and subject to the constraints entailed by human rights. I presented the main arguments in support of this position in chapter 3. I will deal with the implications of this position in greater detail in the next chapter.

---

[33] See reports in http://www.tkuma.org.il/last_news.asp?id=895; http://www.nfc.co.il/archive/001-D-109825-00.html?tag=20-52-32;http://www.kibush.co.il/show_file.asp?num=3784 (all reports are in Hebrew, accessed 6/26/2007).

5

Jewish Hegemony in Immigration and Other Domains

In chapter 3, I argued that Israel's conception of itself as a Jewish state should be far more modest than it is in practice. For reasons stemming from Israel's interpretation of the general notion of the right to self-determination, the practices of many other nation-states around the world, the lessons learned from the persecution of the Jews and from the history of the Jewish-Arab conflict, Israel interprets the Jews' right to self-determination as conferring the Jewish people "ownership" over the state, or at least as entitling the Jewish people to hegemony therein. I have argued that the principled justification invoked for this interpretation of Jewish self-determination, namely, that stemming from the right to self-determination, cannot be used to justify ethnocultural hegemony and that the other three justifications for Jewish hegemony are circumstantial and of limited validity. Jewish self-determination must be realized in Israel and the persecution of the Jews and the conflict with the Palestinians and the Arabs provide circumstantial justification for Jewish hegemony in the areas of security and demography (that is, the numerical balance between the Jewish and Arab populations). Nonetheless, this justification does not extend to the hegemony and even exclusivity that the Jews in Israel have assumed in many other fields. Furthermore, even with regard to demography, the measures that should be adopted to realize and preserve the right to self-determination and Jewish hegemony are limited. The purpose of this chapter is to elaborate on all of these matters.

My concern will primarily be with the normative aspects of the demographic issue and of nationality-based priorities in immigration to Israel. These issues have always been critical to Zionism, both in terms of how it viewed the relationship between Jewish self-determination in the Land of Israel and the Jewish diaspora and in terms of how it thought Jewish self-determination in Israel would impact the fate of the land's indigenous Arab population. The Zionist movement aspired to establish a national home for the Jews in the Land of Israel. Given the fact that most Jews were spread all over the world, Jewish immigration to Israel was essential to achieving this goal.[1] Facilitating Jewish immigration to the Land of Israel thus constituted the core of Zionist ideology, together with the tenet that this land is the only location for realizing Jewish self-determination. However, just as the Zionist movement was divided with respect to the institutional form of self-determination—whether the Jews would have a spiritual center, a substatist political unit, or a state in the Land of Israel—and what the size of the territory for the Jewish national home should be, it was also divided over the demographic objectives of the Jewish return to the Land of Israel and the dimensions of this return.[2]

[1] It may perhaps be necessary to distinguish two senses in which Jewish immigration to the Land of Israel has been an essential and defining element in Zionist ideology. The first sense relates to the realization of Jewish self-determination in the Land of Israel, which was almost empty of Jews at the inception of Zionism, and the rectification of the state of affairs in which the Jews had not realized their self-determination prior to immigrating to Palestine. The second sense refers to nationality-based priorities in immigration arising from the right to self-determination as an issue that pertains to distributive and synchronic justice rather than corrective and diachronic justice. In the latter sense, there is no difference between Zionism and any other nationalism. I will discuss nationality-based priorities in immigration in this second sense later in this chapter.

The refusal of groups such as Agudat Brit Shalom and, later, Agudat 'Ihud (which were peace-seeking groups of Jewish intellectuals in Palestine active in the late 1920s and early 1930s and in the 1940s, respectively; among their members were Martin Buber and Gershom Shcolem) to give up the idea of Jewish immigration to Palestine seems to support the claim that Jewish immigration constitutes a core element in Zionist ideology. During the 25 critical years preceding the establishment of the State of Israel, both of these groups propagated a version of Zionist ideology that was far more modest than that of any other group. They were willing to accept restrictions on Jewish immigration, but were not prepared to relinquish the Jewish right to immigrate to the Land of Israel altogether. To a large extent, the positions that I will present on the issue of immigration in this chapter resemble the positions held by members of these organizations. On the positions of Brit Shalom, 'Ihud, and their members on these issues, see Yosef Gorny, *Zionism and the Arabs, 1882–1948: A Study of Ideology*, trans. Chaya Galai (Oxford: Clarendon, 1987), 118–128, 146, 189–201, 281–289.

[2] The disputes concerning all three dimensions of Zionist aspirations are interwoven. At first blush, it appears that the subscribers to a modest position on the institutional form of Jewish self-determination in the Land of Israel should also have held modest positions on the territorial and demographic dimensions of Zionism. But this did not turn out to be the case. For example, during the 1930s and 1940s, Hashomer Hatzair never sought to institutionalize self-determination in the form of a Jewish nation-state. Hashomer Hatzair aspired to a binational state, although it believed that the entire Jewish people should come to live in the Land of Israel and that Jews should live all over the Land of Israel. Hashomer Hatzair therefore strongly objected to the Peel partition plan. The reverse is also true. That is, at first glance, it

I have already alluded to the two major controversies on this issue. One concerns the question of whether Zionism should aim for the in-gathering of all Jews in the Land of Israel or only for the return of some of the Jewish people to the Land of Israel.[3] The other controversy pertains

---

would appear that those who held ambitious positions with regard to the institutional dimen-sion of Jewish self-determination in Palestine should also have espoused far-reaching positions regarding the territorial and demographic dimensions of Jewish self-determination. But again, as evidenced by the controversies on the issue of partition from 1937 until Ariel Sharon led the disengagement from the Gaza Strip in August 2005 (which is when this chapter was written), the reverse has frequently been true. Except for Jabotinsky and his followers, it is precisely those who are in favor of realizing Jewish self-determination in the form of a hegemonic Jewish state who are also willing to compromise on the territorial dimension of Jewish self-determination. On the debate that took place on these issues in 1937, see Shmuel Dothan, *Partition of Eretz-Israel in the Mandatory Period: The Jewish Controversy* (Jerusalem: Yad Izhak Ben-Zvi, 1979), 16–23 (Hebrew); and Itzhak Galnoor, *Territorial Partition: Decision Crossroads in the Zionist Movement* (Jerusalem: Magnes, 1994), 128–136 (Hebrew).

[3] This is a dispute that also pertains to another controversy dating back to the early days of Zionism and the 1930s over the question of whether it was the role of Zionism to solve what Ahad Ha'am termed "the problem of the Jews" (namely, the economic and social hard-ships of individual Jews) or the "problem of Judaism" (namely, the problems of Jewish identity and the continued existence of the Jews as a people). Not many of the Zionist thinkers, leaders, and parties were consistent or serious in maintaining that it was imperative for the entire Jew-ish people or even the majority of Jews to gather in the Land of Israel. Many of them argued that only a part of the Jewish people would actually immigrate to the Land of Israel. Regarding the diaspora communities, the historian Shimon Dubnow, a prominent non-Zionist Jewish nationalist, contended that the diaspora communities would continue to exist as centers of Jewish culture of equal importance to that in Palestine. See Dothan, *Partition of Eretz-Israel in the Mandatory Period*, 236.

Others argued that centers of Jewish culture outside the Land of Israel would continue to exist but would draw their strength from the Jewish community in Palestine. This is the main thrust of Ahad Ha'am's position. American Zionism as conceived by Louis Brandeis was in some ways similar to Ahad Ha'am's Zionist ideology. Both proclaimed the continued exis-tence of the Jewish diaspora as one of the tenets of their Zionist ideology. American Zionism conceived of the Jewish nation as comprising both a diaspora and the community living in the Land of Israel, with the latter considered to be a cultural center for the Jewish people. See Israel Kolatt, "Eretz Yisrael as a Focus of Dissent and Agreement between Zionists and Anti-Zion-ists," in Haim Avni and Gideon Shimoni (eds.), *Zionism and Its Jewish Opponents* (Jerusalem: Hassifriya Haziyonit, 1990), 21–47, especially 42–43 (Hebrew). Some Zionist thinkers believed that the diaspora would disappear due to Jewish immigration to Palestine and due to the assim-ilation of those who remained in the diaspora. This position is also implicit in Herzl's thinking: "The 'assimilated' would profit even more than Christian citizens by the departure of faithful Jews; for they would be rid of the disquieting, incalculable, and unavoidable rivalry of a Jewish proletariat" (Theodor Herzl, *The Jewish State,* trans. Sylvie d'Avigdor [New York: Dover, 1988], 80). Pinsker also thought that only Jews who were "the inassimilable residue, [will be] removed and elsewhere provided for," that is, in an autonomous Jewish state (Leo Pinsker, *Autoemancipa-tion: An Appeal to His People* [New York: ZOA, 1948], 22). In the introductory statement in the

to whether Jewish self-determination in the Land of Israel necessitates a Jewish majority in that country.[4]

As implied in chapter 3, it is my position that the relationship between the Jews in Israel and the Jews living in the diaspora does not necessarily require that all Jews immigrate to Israel. The substatist interpretation of

---

proposals submitted by the Zionists at the Paris peace conference in February 1919, the Zionist representatives explicitly admitted (section 3) that the Land of Israel was not big enough to contain more than a fraction of the world's Jews and that the majority of Jews living around the world should stay where they were currently living. Indeed, the introduction also referred to the role that the Jewish national home should play with regard to these diaspora Jews. See Ben Halpern, *The Idea of the Jewish State*, 2nd ed. (Cambridge, MA: Harvard University Press, 1969), 297. Those who argued (in a completely different period, that of the partition debate in 1937) that the majority of the Jewish people should gather in the Land of Israel were Jabotinsky (Galnoor, *Territorial Partition*, 173), Yitzhak Tabenkin (ibid., 160), and the leaders of Hashomer Hatzair (ibid., 128), but presumably some of them only subscribed to this view in the context of the predicament in which the Jews found themselves in Europe during the 1930s. This was Ben-Gurion's position at the time. See Gideon Shimoni, *The Zionist Ideology* (Hanover, NH: Brandeis University Press, 1995), 380–381, 383–384. Yechezkel Kaufmann also argued that all Jews should gather in the Land of Israel. This was his position when the partition controversy erupted in 1936–1937 (Dothan, *Partition of Eretz-Israel in the Mandatory Period*, 257–258), and it also follows from his principled positions in *Exile and Foreign Land* (Tel Aviv: Dvir, 1930) (Hebrew) especially vol. 2, chaps. 9 and 10. For other positions on the relationship between Israel and the diaspora, both numerically and in terms of their relative prominence in Zionist thinking in different periods, see Yosef Gorny, *The State of Israel in Jewish Public Thought: The Quest for Collective Identity* (New York: New York University Press, 1994), particularly chap. 10 and the book's afterword. To the best of my knowledge, the main ideologue favoring the elimination of the Jewish diaspora in the last 30 years is Yehoshua. This can be seen in his essay about the Jewish *Golah* (exile), "The *Golah*: The Neurotic Solution," in A. B. Yehoshua, *Between Right and Right*, trans. Arnold Schwartz (Garden City, NY: Doubleday, 1981), 21–74, especially, for example, 60–62, and also in his essay on anti-Semitism, "An Attempt to Identify and Understand the Foundations of Anti-Semitism," *Alpayim* 28 (2005), 11–30 (Hebrew).

[4] Unlike the numerical relationship between the Jews living in the Land of Israel and the Jews of the diaspora, with regard to which there is no clear Zionist consensus, there is certainly general agreement among Zionists regarding the desirable proportion between the Jews and the Arabs in Palestine. Most Zionists supported the goal of securing a Jewish majority in the Land of Israel. The only exceptions to this were the members of Brit Shalom and their successors in the 'Ihud, who waived this demand and supported the goal of establishing Jewish settlements all over the Land of Israel, but did not necessarily call for a Jewish majority. See Gorny, *Zionism and the Arabs*, 121–122, on Rabbi Benjamin's (the pen name of essayist Joshua Redler-Feldman) position (he wished to see many Jews living in the Land of Israel, even if they did not constitute a majority, as opposed to the view that emphasizes the need to attain a majority). On Ernest Simon's position, see 192, and on the position of the 'Ihud, particularly Martin Buber, see 284. All of them waived the demand for a majority. Gorny notes that even Weizmann, just before the 17th Zionist Congress, did not insist on having a Jewish majority (192). However, he was criticized for this by the moderate Zionist leadership. Gorny further points out that, at the beginning of the 1930s, Buber quoted comments made by Yosef Sprinzak

the right to self-determination for which I argued is also interstatist and assumes the continued existence of national diasporas. The members of these diasporas have an interest in the continued existence and preservation of their original culture. However, this interest could be nurtured by means of the realization of the national group's self-determination even if not all of the members of any given group move to the homeland. In this chapter, I will include more specific arguments against the aspiration that all Jews should gather in Israel.

My position on the issue of the numerical balance between Jews and non-Jews in Israel is more complex. Indeed, the mainstream position of Zionism has always been that there should be a Jewish majority in the Land of Israel. However, there were a few prominent Zionist figures who held a different view.[5] As entailed by my discussion in chapter 3, the realization of the right to national self-determination does not itself require the existence of a Jewish majority in the Land of Israel. Rather, it requires the existence of a Jewish community in numbers that would enable the members of that community to live most aspects of their lives, including their economic and political lives, within the framework of their culture. On the other hand, the persecution of the Jews and the Jewish-Palestinian conflict justify the aspiration to maintain a Jewish majority in Israel. However, this justification is only circumstantially legitimate and should be viewed as temporary since, from a moral perspective, it is incumbent upon all those involved to bring an end to persecution, to the violent conflict between the Jews and the Palestinians, and to the related psychological repercussions of these phenomena.

(who would become the first Speaker of the Knesset after the State of Israel was established) that were similar to those made by Weizmann (284). Regarding Ahad Ha'am, it is obvious that he did not feel that it was necessary for all Jews or even most Jews to gather in Palestine. And yet, in his article "Three Steps," he speaks of the goal of securing a Jewish "majority" (his quotation marks) in the Land of Israel (*The Writings of Ahad Ha'am* [Tel Aviv: Dvir, 1947], 153 [Hebrew]). Nevertheless, it could be argued that, in referring to a "majority," Ahad Ha'am did not necessarily mean a majority in the country as a whole, but rather to areas in which Jews would constitute the majority. This interpretation is substantiated by his other comments in the same article. For example, he cites the three national groups in Switzerland, noting that each of these national groups is a majority in only one part of Switzerland and can therefore lead a "national life" there. This interpretation of Ahad Ha'am's notion of "majority" is also compatible with the view he expresses in the epigraph at the beginning of this book (see p. 3) as well as with his general conception of the objectives of Zionism, namely, the establishment of a spiritual center for the Jewish people in Palestine.

[5] See previous note.

Irrespective of whether the appropriate demographic objective of Zionism is the existence of a Jewish presence in Israel in numbers sufficient to allow its members to live in the framework of their culture, or the existence of a Jewish majority, the important normative issues regarding these demographic objectives pertain primarily to the legitimate means for the realization of these goals. Israel's principal means for realizing these objectives thus far have been its Law of Return and its Citizenship Law. These laws grant every Jew anywhere in the world the right to immigrate to Israel and become a citizen of the State of Israel.[6] Many liberals and left-wingers consider these laws to be tainted with racism, because they view any nationality-based preference in immigration as a form of racism. In section 1, I will argue against this position. I will then offer three justifications for nationality-based preferences in immigration. However, the fact that nationality-based priorities in immigration are not necessarily racist and that there are legitimate human interests justifying such priorities does not entail that the specific priorities manifested by Israel's Law of Return and its other immigration and citizenship policies are just. These policies in effect mean that all Jews and only Jews (or anyone related or married to a Jew) have the right to immigrate to Israel and to become fully integrated in Israeli life. In section 3, I will argue that these two aspects of Israel's immigration policies, namely, its almost categorical inclusion of all Jews and its almost categorical exclusion of all non-Jews, are somewhat problematic. In section 4, I will propose three principles for nationality-based priorities in immigration which avoid automatically allowing all Jews to immigrate to Israel and acquire Israeli citizenship and which avoid barring all non-Jews from doing so. The right that the Law of Return grants to every individual Jew to immigrate to Israel was of great symbolic value at the time of its enactment, which was not long after World War II and the establishment of the State of Israel. This symbolic value presumably still holds sway. However, I will argue that the present-day reality in Israel requires immigration policies that are less ethnocentric and more universal.

In addition to the Law of Return, a number of additional ways to ultimately increase the number of Jews in relation to the number of Arabs have been proposed and even adopted in Israel. During the incumbency of the

---

[6] The Law of Return, 5710/1950, was amended in 1970 to apply not only to Jews but also to non-Jewish spouses of Jews, or children or grandchildren of Jews and their spouses. The Citizenship Law, 5712/1952, allows those who have immigrated to Israel under the Law of Return to receive citizenship almost automatically.

15th Knesset, right-wing Member of Knesset Michael Kleiner introduced a draft bill intended "to encourage people that do not identify with the Jewish character of the state [i.e., Palestinian citizens of Israel] to leave."[7] The Israeli government later introduced a bill—which was passed—to amend the Israeli Citizenship Law in a manner that would deny Arabs who are Israeli citizens and who have married Palestinian residents of the occupied territories the right to live in Israel with their spouses and children.[8] In section 5, I will clarify why both of these laws, namely, Kleiner's law and the law pertaining to family unification, are racist, whereas granting Jews priority in immigration is not. In section 6 of this chapter, I will briefly discuss other hegemonic laws and practices in Israel pertaining to land, education, political participation, state symbols, the national anthem, names of places and institutions, and the main official language. All of these laws and practices are intended to promote or express the state's Jewish identity in a manner that discriminates against and even excludes all non-Jews.

1. NATIONALITY-BASED IMMIGRATION AND RACISM

Many Israelis who regard the Law of Return to be a racist law do so because they believe that any distinction based on race, nationality, or ethnic origin is racist. They draw support for this interpretation of racism from the opening words of Article 1 of the UN International Convention on the Elimination of All Forms of Racial Discrimination, according to which the term "racial discrimination" applies to "any distinction, exclusion, restriction or preference based on race, color, descent, or national or ethnic origin." Indeed, Article 1 provides a very broad definition of racism. In section 5, I will argue that even this broad definition of racism does not really apply to the nationalist preferences embodied by the Law of Return. However, at this stage, I will not deal with the appropriate interpretation of Article 1, but will instead discuss the claim that any distinction based on race, descent,

---

[7] Kleiner's bill, entitled A Bill to Encourage Emigration to Arab States, 5761/2001, was not included in *The Official Gazette: Bills* apparently because the Knesset presidency had disqualified it so that it could not be submitted as a subject to be debated in the Knesset plenum.

[8] The Citizenship and Entry into Israel Law (Temporary Provision), 5763/2003. The law was passed on August 6, 2003. Its validity was temporary, but it has been extended several times. In May 2006, a 6–5 majority of the High Court of Justice rejected a petition challenging the constitutionality of this law (HCJ 7052/03, *Adalah—The Legal Center for Arab Minority Rights in Israel v. The Minister of Interior* [Hebrew]).

nationality, or ethnic origin is racist. I will also address the argument often voiced in Israel that the Law of Return is nevertheless justified as a form of affirmative action. This argument necessarily presupposes that the Law of Return is racist. However, the proponents of this argument also believe that, as in other cases of affirmative action, the particular racism of the Law of Return is justified and that the State of Israel and the Zionist movement may indeed invoke the Law of Return in order to redress the racist evils and deprivations which Jews suffered in the past.

A proponent of these views is the Israeli philosopher Asa Kasher. According to him, if a national group has been deprived of the conditions that would have allowed it to realize its self-determination, it ought now to be permitted to become a majority in a given territory, thus attaining the conditions necessary for self-determination.[9] Kasher therefore argues for a principle he calls "the case of the founding fathers," which he believes to be derived from the right to national self-determination. This principle asserts the right of individuals belonging to a national group to immigrate into a territory in numbers sufficient for the realization of their right to self-determination, which, according to Kasher, means becoming a majority in that territory. The case of the founding fathers constitutes a nationality-based preference. Kasher views such a preference as racist.[10] However, he also believes that affirmative action justifies this preference in the same way that, for example, it permits discrimination in favor of African Americans and/or women in university or employment quotas, even though this preferential treatment is actually based on race and/or gender. This bias is considered justified as a temporary means to rectify the consequences of the injustices suffered by African Americans and by women. Similarly, the nationality-based priorities created by the case of the founding fathers are

---

[9] Asa Kasher, "Justice and Affirmative Action: Naturalization and the Law of Return," *Israel Yearbook on Human Rights* 15 (1985), 101–112.

[10] In pages 103–106 of his article, Kasher rejects the claim that nationality-based preferences are not racist if a country does not apply them to its own citizens but to potential immigrants only. The UN Convention on the Elimination of All Forms of Racial Discrimination includes a provision to this effect. In my view, Kasher's reasons for rejection of this possibility are sound. See my discussion in Gans, *The Limits of Nationalism*, 125–127. In this context, it ought to be noted that many philosophers and political theorists have debated the question of whether the notion of justice applies merely within specific states, or whether it also applies globally. Many theorists have worked out the implications of these different approaches with regard to immigration. Some seminal writings on this topic are Michael Walzer's *Spheres of Justice* (Oxford: Blackwell, 1983), chap. 2; and Joseph H. Carens, "Aliens and Citizens: The Case for Open Borders," *Review of Politics* 49 (1987), 251–273.

claimed to be temporarily justified until the injustice suffered by the Jews with regard to their right to self-determination is rectified, that is, until they constitute a majority in their country.[11]

One obvious reason for objecting to nationality-based immigration priorities as a kind of affirmative action, at least in the case of the Jews in Israel, is that those who are required to pay the price for it are the Palestinians, who are not responsible for Jewish suffering in the past. This is in contrast to African Americans and women in the United States, who are currently favored at the expense of whites and men, respectively. Unlike Palestinians in Israel, whites or men as a group are indeed guilty of having discriminated against African Americans or women in the past. However, there are more fundamental considerations that preclude regarding the priorities established by the Law of Return as a case of affirmative action rectifying earlier wrongs. These considerations derive from the fact that affirmative action only pertains to advantages granted to members of groups *whose membership in these particular groups is in principle irrelevant to any privileges currently accorded to these groups*. Advocates of affirmative action for African Americans and women in higher education and employment in the United States also believe that race and gender should not in principle affect a person's educational or career opportunities. The interests that African Americans and women have in education, for example, and the reasons they have for wishing to be educated have nothing to do with their skin color or gender. This point makes it impossible to classify the nationality-based priorities created by the Law of Return (including the priority created under Kasher's founding fathers interpretation) as affirmative action. Compensating members of the Jewish people for the deprivation they suffered with regard to their interest in self-determination pertains to a matter to which their Jewishness is relevant. If they deserve compensation in this matter, then it cannot be classified as affirmative action. In other words, in acknowledging a people's legitimate interest in its own self-determination as a national group, one necessarily subscribes to the view that nationality-based priorities are not necessarily racist, and therefore nationality-based immigration priorities intended to serve this interest are not necessarily racist. At least, they are not racist in the primary sense of this term.

According to the primary sense of racism (to be distinguished from the sense defined by Article 1 of the Convention on the Elimination of Racial

---

[11] Kasher, "Justice and Affirmative Action," 112.

Discrimination, which will be discussed below), distinctions between people are racist if they are based on membership in the groups to which people belong by birth or upbringing and if these distinctions are invoked for purposes unrelated to the particular group membership. Discriminating against doctors and in favor of lawyers in determining their income tax is not racist because it does not satisfy the first condition. That is, it does not apply to people by virtue of their membership in groups to which they belong due to birth or upbringing. Similarly, decisions favoring of blacks as potential candidates for the role of Othello, tall people in choosing candidates for a basketball team, or handicapped people in distributing parking spaces are not racist decisions because they do not satisfy the second condition. This form of discrimination is based on involuntary membership in groups but is relevant to the legitimate purposes for which it is invoked. For the same reason, people who acknowledge the legitimacy of the right to national self-determination would not consider nationality-based immigration priorities invoked for the purpose of implementing this right as necessarily racist, at least not in the sense under consideration here.

Rejecting Israel's Law of Return as a case of affirmative action does not preclude the possibility of justifying it on grounds of ordinary remedial considerations. It must be remembered that affirmative action is a particular type of remedy for the rectification of racial or quasi-racial injustices. This is achieved by means of "reverse racism." Just as racial injustices are not the only type of injustice, reverse racism is not the only way (and for the most part, not even the most appropriate way) to provide a remedy for racial injustice. Just as it is justified to discontinue the imprisonment of a group of black people arrested merely because of their race and to compensate them for false arrest, though not necessarily by means of reverse racism (for example, by refraining from arresting them in the future even if they do commit crimes and possibly also by the wrongful arrest of whites), it may have been justified to terminate the Jewish people's exile from their homeland, which had resulted in disastrous persecution. In chapter 2, I resorted to this claim in order to justify Zionist aspirations for a Jewish return to the Land of Israel for the realization of Jewish self-determination. I argued that considerations of distributive justice entitled the Jewish people to realize their self-determination, and their historical rights entitled them to select the site of this self-determination in the Land of Israel. This, however, is true only from the perspective of ideal global justice. In our non-ideal world, acting on such considerations should be suspended. I also argued that the persecution of the Jews created a situation which nevertheless justified the realization of their right of self-determination, despite the fact that the ensuing injustice and bloodshed was expected. It thus follows that the principle referred to by Kasher as the case of the founding fathers might, in certain cases, be relied upon as a remedy. The historical circumstances faced by the Jews, at least following the Nazi rise to power, can indeed be said to constitute a legitimate situation for invoking this principle.

However, if nationality-based priorities may occasionally be justified by remedial considerations, such as the urgent need created by persecution, then cases justified by considerations of ordinary justice unrelated to remedying such emergency situations are also conceivable. Justified remedies necessarily presuppose primary rights. These remedies are meant to rectify violations of the primary rights. For example, the right to compensation for bodily damage presupposes some sort of primary right to bodily integrity. If the persecution of the Jews justified their return to their original homeland and the realization of their primary right to self-determination there, then this right to self-determination—from the moment it was exercised—may also have justified continued Jewish immigration, but for other reasons that do not only pertain to one-time events. These reasons derive from the need to protect the primary right to self-determination (just as the primary right to bodily integrity justifies other permanent rights, such as the right not to be attacked). My main concern here is with justifying the Law of Return in the current situation in which the Jews already enjoy self-determination and do not have as acute a need to escape persecution. Under these conditions, the Law of Return can no longer be justified by remedial considerations. Rather, it must be justified by resorting to primary rights and the way they should be protected.

2. SELF-DETERMINATION AND NATIONALITY-BASED PRIORITIES IN IMMIGRATION

I would like to argue now that national priorities in immigration could be derived from the right to national self-determination and that anyone recognizing this right for the reasons justifying it from the liberal perspective must also be committed to recognizing priorities in immigration for members of national groups.

One justification for the right to self-determination which also justifies granting priorities in immigration to members of a national group desiring to immigrate to their homeland is the interest that members of national groups have in adhering to their cultures, flourishing within the frameworks of their cultures, and sustaining them for generations. Another justification for self-determination, which at the same time also justifies nationality-based priorities in immigration, is that members of groups with a history of persecution might wish for their culture to thrive, since it provides a source of self-respect and since a community of their own may help them to protect themselves. If these interests do indeed justify the continued existence and the self-rule of national groups, then they certainly justify granting priorities in immigration to members of these groups. If the right to self-rule is intended to protect the interests of members of national groups in adhering to their cultures and living within the frameworks of their cultures, there is no point in recognizing this right unless one also acknowledges the desire of members of these groups to immigrate to their homelands in order to realize their desire to live within their cultures' frameworks (as opposed to a desire to immigrate for economic reasons, for example). By the same token, if the reason that many national groups strive for self-determination is to provide a safe haven from persecution and to instill a general sense of security, there is no point in recognizing this right unless one also recognizes the right of individual members of these groups to find refuge from persecution in their homelands.

The third justification which I wish to suggest for nationality-based priorities in immigration derives from the fact that such priorities serve the interests of all members of the group, and not only the immigrants themselves, in maintaining the framework of their culture and in its self-rule, regardless of whether they are living in the diaspora or in the country where the group has realized its self-determination. For example, regardless of whether they happen to be living in Turkey or in Germany, Turks may have an interest in maintaining the continuous existence of their group and in realizing its self-determination in their homeland. The same could be said to apply to Algerians, regardless of whether they are living in Algeria or in France, or to Jews, irrespective of whether they are living in Israel or anywhere else in the world. If this interest justifies the right to self-determination, it would seem that, subject to moral constraints, it must also justify auxiliary rights to carry out the necessary actions required to maintain that self-determination. If the size of the group is liable to decrease to numbers insufficient to ensure its members' ability to flourish in the framework of their culture, allowing diaspora members to move to where the national group has realized its self-determination and to become citizens of this state could be such an action. In some native reservations in North America, even more radical means are employed for this very purpose. Not only are Native Americans granted a special right to move to these reservations, but anyone who does not belong to this group is almost never allowed to move to these reservations.[12] In the case of the native minorities of North America, I believe these two practices to be justified. If there are circumstances that justify both the inclusion of members and the exclusion of nonmembers, then it is certainly conceivable that there may be circumstances justifying only inclusion, that is, establishing nationality-based priorities in immigration for the purpose of preserving the group on a scale that enables its members to continue living and prospering within the framework of their culture.

The right to national self-determination is clearly a significant collective right. It is a significant right not only in terms of the important individual interests which it protects but also in terms of the burdens and responsibilities it places on people, states, and the international community as a whole. To a great extent, it determines world order. If the interests that people have in adhering to their culture and in preserving it for future generations justify measures that affect world order, then it would seem that these considerations could also justify recognizing certain nationality-based preferential treatment in immigration. It seems logically and morally inconsistent to argue that these interests justify the collective right to self-determination but do not justify nationality-based priorities in immigration.

Many liberals object to nationality-based priorities in immigration not only because they consider them to be racist, but also because they regard them as incompatible with the ideal of state neutrality and because they produce what seem to be two unequal classes of citizens. They also claim that such priorities violate the principle of equality among individuals in the name of a collective right and thus conflict with the liberal principle of the moral primacy of individuals over collective entities. The claim that national preferences in immigration violate the ideal of neutrality and create two unequal classes of citizens is factually correct. But, as I already clarified in chapter 1, it is doubtful whether such infringements of neutrality and equality are problematic. In practice, it is impossible for countries whose populations speak many different languages to realize the ideals of neutrality and equality with regard to culture, nor is it clear whether, from the liberal point of view, it is desirable for such countries to aspire to realize these

---

[12] For a description of the special rights that the First Nations have in their reservations in Canada, see Will Kymlicka, *Liberalism, Community and Culture* (Oxford: Clarendon, 1989), chap. 7.

ideals in the realm of culture.[13] If it is in practice impossible for states with heterogeneous populations to be culturally neutral, then this may indeed indicate that the ideal of cultural equality may be one to be aimed at on the global level rather than on the state level. This would mean that different cultural groups would enjoy certain types of special privileges in different parts of the world, so that each group has at least one place in which its culture is maintained and continues to flourish and where the people belonging to this culture can live within its framework. In this particular place, the culture would enjoy special privileges; among other things, the language of this particular ethnocultural group would be granted official status, and members of this group would be preferred for immigration into the country.[14]

The claim that nationality-based preferences in immigration express the ideological precedence of collective entities over individuals and are therefore incompatible with liberalism[15] should be rejected because the immigration preferences in question do not really imply that collective interests precede individual interests. According to the liberal interpretation of the collective right to self-determination, this right is not one that derives from collective interests. Rather, it is based mainly on individual interests, namely, those that individuals have in adhering to their culture, in maintaining its existence, and in its flourishing in the future.[16] Nationality-based priorities in immigration serve to promote the right to self-determination. In order to achieve this purpose, they are structured so as to preserve a demographic minimum whereby individuals belonging to a cultural group

[13] See Will Kymlicka, "Western Political Theory and Ethnic Relations in Eastern Europe," in Will Kymlicka and Magda Opalski (eds.), *Can Liberal Pluralism Be Exported? Western Political Theory and Ethnic Relations in Eastern Europe* (Oxford: Oxford University Press, 2001), 13–106, especially 16–21.

[14] For a more detailed discussion, see Chaim Gans, *The Limits of Nationalism* (Cambridge: Cambridge University Press, 2003), 83–91.

[15] For a similar criticism concerning language rights, see, for example, Brian Barry on the Quebec government's requirement that Canadian Anglophone migrants from other provinces should send their children to French-speaking schools in Quebec rather than choose an English-language educational setting. The government justified this requirement by invoking the need to preserve Quebec's Francophone culture. Brian Barry, *Culture and Equality: An Egalitarian Critique of Multiculturalism* (Cambridge: Polity, 2001), 65–68. See also the remarks by Jürgen Habermas, "Recognition and Redistribution: What Does It Take to Reproduce a Culture," *Tel Aviv University Law Review* 27 (2003), 11–21 (Hebrew).

[16] See Joseph Raz, *The Morality of Freedom* (Oxford: Oxford University Press, 1986), 207–209.

can continue to live most aspects of their lives within the framework of their culture. These preferences also serve the interstatist dimension of the right to self-determination, namely, that which protects the interests that members of national diasporas might have in the continued existence of their original culture and in its self-determination. What this means is that nationality-based priorities in immigration are an auxiliary means for the realization of the collective right to self-determination and are therefore not incompatible with the liberal precedence of the individual over the collective. In the final analysis, the justification for nationality-based priorities in immigration derives from interests that individual human beings have in the existence and in the self-determination of their group.

To sum up, the justifications for nationality-based preferences in immigration are not limited to considerations of diachronic justice and the need to remedy the wrongs of the past but also include considerations of synchronic justice and the need to fulfill fundamental and enduring human interests. One must reject the claim that the incompatibility of the Law of Return with the liberal ideals of neutrality and equality renders it unjust. Nonetheless, this does not mean that the Law of Return and Israel's other immigration and citizenship policies are just, for indeed they are not, as I will demonstrate in the next section of this chapter.

3. Immigration to Israel: All Jews and Only Jews

The Law of Return grants every Jew from anywhere in the world the right to immigrate to Israel. The Citizenship Law allows those who have immigrated to Israel under the Law of Return to receive citizenship almost automatically. According to the Citizenship Law, there are almost no other ways to attain Israeli citizenship. The fact that the Law of Return is the only law that addresses the issue of immigration to Israel means there is virtually no way for non-Jews to immigrate to Israel.[17] In effect, Israel is open to all Jews and closed to all non-Jews. The nationality-based priorities in immigration to Israel are thus very different from nationality-based immigration priorities practiced in some other countries. I briefly mentioned this point in chapter 3 when I referred to Yakobson and Rubinstein's attempt to mobilize support for Israel's Law of Return by citing the immigration practices in other countries. Most countries that grant special rights regarding immigration and naturalization to members of their main ethnocultural group—such

---

[17] Unless they are relatives of Jews. See note 6.

as Finland, Germany, and Greece—do not do so by granting an individual right to all members of their diasporas to immigrate, and they certainly do not limit immigration and naturalization solely to members of their own ethnocultural group. Germany only grants priorities in immigration and naturalization to those ethnic Germans who are refugees or have been expelled from where they formerly resided. At least in the purely legal sense (as opposed to cultural integration), Germany has not excluded all potential immigrants whose original culture is not German. Similarly, at the beginning of the 1990s, after the collapse of the Soviet Union, Finland granted ethnic Finns residing across the Russian border the right to immigrate to Finland and receive citizenship. The special immigration privileges granted to ethnic Finns after the collapse of the Soviet Union in the 1990s were designed for a group of people who suffered under Soviet rule and who suddenly found themselves in a politically volatile situation.[18] Finland does not grant ethnic Finns a universal right to immigrate and be naturalized, and it certainly does not have immigration and naturalization policies that deny those who are not ethnic Finns the option of immigrating and integrating into the country. In Greece and Italy, anyone of Greek or Italian origin, respectively, is granted priority in immigration and naturalization. However, in both countries, it is not only Greeks or Italians that may immigrate or attain citizenship. As stated above, the Law of Return grants all Jews a universal right to immigrate to Israel, and it is virtually impossible for anyone who is not Jewish or who does not have kinship ties with Jews to receive Israeli citizenship.

As noted earlier, both the unrestricted admission of Jews and the complete exclusion of non-Jews are problematic. With regard to the former, state authorities should at least have some discretion in making decisions regarding immigration policies. Any decisions made by the authorities should express their primary responsibility toward the country's citizens and their current needs. In granting categorical immigration rights to a large group of potential immigrants, the Law of Return does not leave the state the option of considering whether the country's citizens' current interests really allow for any immigration or how many immigrants should be admitted. This is problematic, both in itself and also because it implies that the immigration interests of a group of people from outside the country have absolute priority over the interests of the citizens of the

---

[18] See Emma Nurmela, "Repaying the Debt of Honor: Ingrian Immigration to Finland," available at: http://www.uta.fi/FAST/FIN/HIST/en-ingim.html (accessed 6/26/2007).

country. This means that the ordinary interests of the country's citizens do not count vis-à-vis those of members of the diaspora group in immigrating. This should concern both Jewish and Arab Israeli citizens, because like all governments, the Israeli government should not totally relinquish the right to exercise discretion with regard to its immigration policies as required by the particular socioeconomic circumstances in the country at any given time. With regard to Jewish Israeli citizens, this concern is perhaps mitigated by the fact that these absolute immigration rights were instituted in the name of their ethnocultural interests. This is not the case with regard to the Arab citizens of Israel. The fact that the government relinquishes all discretion regarding Jewish immigration into Israel means that any related interests that Israel's Arab citizens might have are entirely disregarded.[19]

In addition to these principled objections to Israel's absolute openness toward all Jews under the Law of Return, this universal admission of Jews also raises some significant practical problems. It poses real demographic threats to Israeli Jews and certainly to Arabs, whether Israeli citizens, residents of the occupied territories, or perhaps also Arabs living in neighboring countries. Arab anxiety is especially acute because the history of Zionism is replete with cases where Arabs were uprooted and dispossessed as a result of Jewish immigration. Recently, however, the Law of Return has also kindled anxiety among Jews living in Israel, who fear an unlimited influx of immigrants who would impinge on many aspects of their lives. The following are cases that have aggravated these feelings of anxiety. Many Ethiopians have demanded the right to immigrate to Israel on the basis of their kinship ties with Falasha (Ethiopian) Jews; many undesirable criminals from the Commonwealth of Independent States (CIS) have in recent years infiltrated Israel; and several large population groups in Africa and India have recently claimed to be of Jewish origin.[20] What all of this boils down

---

[19] The point could be explained in terms of Kant's humanity formula of the categorical imperative: Act in such a way that humanity is never treated simply as a means but always also as an end. If the state relinquishes its right to consider the interests of its Jewish citizens in favor of the interests of Jews who are not citizens in immigrating to it, then the former are being used as a means to serve the interests of the latter. But since this is not only done in the name of the interest that diaspora Jews have in immigrating to Israel, but also in the name of the ethnocultural interests of the Jewish citizens of the state, the latter do not merely serve to fulfill the needs of others. Their own needs are also considered. They are thus also treated as an end. This does not apply to the Arab citizens of Israel.

[20] These groups do not share a history, culture, or traditions with most other groups of Jews who immigrated to Israel. According to various political factions wishing to further

to is that even though there are reasons that justify granting priority to Jewish immigration to Israel, they do not require that the Law of Return be formulated in such a way as to unconditionally allow all Jews to immigrate to Israel and subsequently attain citizenship.

Let me now turn to the exclusion of non-Jews from Israel's immigration arrangements, which appears to be even more problematic than the universal inclusion of all Jews under the Law of Return. Until the 1990s, there were few non-Jews who wished to immigrate to Israel or become citizens of the country. The practical implications of the policy of excluding non-Jews were therefore limited. However, this changed because of the large influx of non-Jewish labor migrants that began in 1990. Consequently, there is now a substantial group of non-Jews living in Israel.[21] As labor migrants, they have become an integral part of the Israeli economy. Many of these labor migrants have spent many years in Israel. Moreover, their children attend Israeli schools, speak Hebrew, and have become totally acculturated into Israeli society. Many of these children have lost or never had their parents' cultural identity. For a long time, the Israeli government refused to grant these children permanent status. Although there have recently been some changes with regard to the legal status of these children, the general issue of not allowing non-Jews to immigrate to Israel or to acquire permanent status has not really been addressed. In my opinion, this constitutes a callous disregard of the moral obligation emanating from Jewish history and from the fact that the Jewish people is still mainly a diasporic nation.

---

expand Jewish settlements in the West Bank, as well as various romantics in search of the lost tribes of Israel, the former are population groups that supposedly have ancient blood ties to Jews. Even if clear proof of such ties could be found, they have nothing whatsoever to do with the human interests underlying the ideal of national self-determination. The justification for nationality-based priorities in immigration discussed in the previous section of the chapter does not apply to these groups. There is no reason for the Law of Return to be formulated in such a way as to grant them any kind of privileges in immigrating to Israel.

[21] In fact, another major source of non-Jews living in Israel is the mass wave of immigrants who arrived in Israel in the 1990s after the collapse of the Soviet Union. Under Israel's Law of Return and Citizenship Law, they are granted the same immigration and citizenship rights as Jews (see note 6). Obviously, Israel's policies toward this particular group of non-Jews are accommodating. However, this cannot serve to refute the claim that Israel's immigration policies exclude non-Jews; members of the current group are granted the right to immigrate and become citizens only because of their kinship ties with Jews. Moreover, many influential politicians in Israel often demand that the Law of Return be amended so as to make it inapplicable to the non-Jewish relatives of Jews.

Examples of political entities open to all members of a particular group and closed to almost all others are the reservations for native minorities in Canada mentioned earlier. All members of the tribe may move to these reservations, whereas it is virtually impossible for anyone who is not a member of the tribe to move there. In these cases, however, the immigration policy is justified for a number of reasons, inter alia, the desire to preserve the traditional character of the public space in these reservations. This means that, because most tribes are relatively small, it is necessary to prevent people who do not belong to the same culture from moving to the reservation. Israel's policy is like that of a tribal reservation, although there is no real justification for such a policy, for the Jewish group in Israel is not as small as a tribe, nor does Israeli culture, economy, and politics resemble those of a reservation. In the next section of this chapter, I will propose three principles for nationality-based priorities in immigration which ought to satisfy the objectives of Jewish self-determination and serve as guidelines for the ethnocultural component of Israel's overall immigration policy.

4. PRINCIPLES FOR NATIONALITY-BASED PRIORITIES IN IMMIGRATION

The guiding principles presented below assume that ethnocultural considerations are only one factor shaping the general principles that ought to guide immigration policies. These principles are intended as a framework for striking a balance between the needs of the ethnocultural groups enjoying self-determination within particular countries and the general needs, which are not necessarily ethnocultural, both of the potential immigrants and of the citizens of these countries. These principles are based on the three justifications for nationality-based priorities in immigration that I presented in section 2 of this chapter: (1) When states attempt to determine immigration policies, the nationality-based motivation of potential immigrants should have considerable weight. States should allot a portion of their immigration quotas to those immigrants who, for nationalist reasons, wish to live where their nation enjoys self-determination; (2) national groups may admit the number of members into their homelands that is required in order for them to maintain their self-determination; and (3) states have a duty to take in refugees and persecuted members of specific national groups that have a right to self-determination within their specific states and also to grant priority to members of these groups within all of the other categories that make up their immigration quotas.

The first of the above three principles is that the nationality-based motivations of potential immigrants should play a significant role in the overall balance of considerations in a country's determination of its immigration policies. This principle is based on the first justification for nationality-based priorities in immigration presented above, which is also a justification for the right to self-determination, namely, the need to serve the interests that many people have in adhering to their culture and in living within their ethnocultural group. According to this principle, countries should award entitlement points to those wishing to immigrate for ethnocultural reasons. However, this principle does not give members of national diasporas a *personal right* to immigrate to the country where their group enjoys national self-determination. The importance of this principle is its recognition of the additional significance that should be ascribed to nationality-based motives within the balance of considerations that determine a country's immigration policies. This balance must also include other types of considerations stemming from any other interests that the potential immigrants might have (for example, their interest in overcoming poverty) and from any interests that the citizens and residents of the target country might have (for example, their need for workers in particular professions). Whether or not the significance of the nationality-based motives of potential immigrants is sufficient for admitting them depends, of course, on specific circumstances.

The first principle clearly implies a position that does not interpret the aspiration of the Zionist movement to bring the Jews to the Land of Israel as necessarily involving the return of all Jews, but rather as aspiring for a partial return of the Jewish people. Similarly, this is true with regard to the other two principles. According to the second principle, within the specific area where a particular national group's right to self-determination is realized, the group is entitled to admit the number of diaspora members sufficient to maintain its right to self-determination. This principle is based on the need to occasionally adopt measures that are necessary for preserving cultures in such a manner that enables their members to live within the framework of their culture and to maintain self-rule. Unlike the first principle, which grants individual advantages to nationally motivated individuals to immigrate to the country in which their national group enjoys self-determination, the advantages conferred by the second principle are conferred to a national group, and not to individuals. As such, advantages conferred under the second principle are not intended to serve potential immigrants' individual interests in immigrating. Rather, they are meant to serve the interests of all members of the national group in the continued existence and self-determination of the group, irrespective of whether they belong to the core group or to the diaspora. This being the case, immigration based on this principle can include members of the national group who do not necessarily wish to immigrate for ethnocultural reasons. It can also include members whose motivations are economic, religious, political, and so forth.

The third guiding principle for nationality-based priorities in immigration posits the obligation incumbent upon states to admit refugees and persecuted members of the national groups that enjoy self-determination within the frameworks of these respective states. Moreover, according to this principle, they are also obligated to give preference to members of these groups in all of the other categories of their immigration quotas. This principle is based on the third justification mentioned above for nationality-based priorities in immigration, namely, the interest that members of ethnocultural groups—especially those with a history of persecution—have in an ethnocultural homeland where they belong. Such a home country, with whose citizens they feel some historic and cultural affinity, provides them with a sense of security and could actually serve as a safe haven in the event of an emergency. Acting in accordance with this principle is an important aspect of national self-determination. It allows national groups living in their homelands, who are the main beneficiaries of the right to self-determination, to demonstrate solidarity and responsibility toward all members of their respective diasporas.[22]

Unlike Israel's Law of Return and its immigration and naturalization policies, these three guiding principles for nationality-based priorities in immigration do not automatically include all Jews and exclude all non-Jews. The Law of Return and the immigration and naturalization arrangements in Israel reflect an ethnocentric view of the right to Jewish self-determination and the Jewish nation-state. It reflects the position that the country is, first and foremost, a tool in the hands of the Jewish ethnocultural group. This position is very prevalent among the Jewish majority in Israel and perhaps also among many non-Israeli Jews. According to this interpretation of Jewish self-determination, all interests that non-Jews might have, including ethnocultural interests, as well as any interests that

---

[22] On particularist obligations emanating from common culture and nationality, see Gans, *The Limits of Nationalism*, chap. 7.

Jews might have other than their ethnocultural interests (for example, their interest in improving their standard of living, or any individual's interest in pursuing a particular professional career) which might conflict with the Jewish interest in self-determination are not taken into account at all. Such an approach is not prevalent in any other country in the world that Israel should want to emulate and is unacceptable in moral terms. Also, in view of the fact that the Jewish people have lived in the diaspora for most of their history, Israel has its own special reasons for not endorsing this approach.

In all fairness, it must be noted that there are many people for whom Jewish history provides compelling reasons for doing the reverse, that is, for actually promoting this ethnocentric conception of Israel. For them, the Law of Return is inextricably bound up with the presumption of an unconditional right for Jews to immigrate to Israel. In the minds of many Israelis, replacing the Law of Return with immigration quotas for Jews based on a point system would immediately evoke associations of practices and concepts in Jewish history from which the establishment of the State of Israel was meant to free the Jews. Two examples that are particularly charged emotionally are the "White Paper" and the *numerus clausus*, both of which have attained a prominent status in the Zionist ethos and have had a formative impact on collective Israeli consciousness. The former refers to restrictions imposed by the British on the entry of Jews into Palestine in 1939. These restrictions were also applied to survivors from Nazi concentration camps. The latter term refers to the admission quota for Jews which was implemented by universities and which also pertained to certain types of jobs in eastern Europe (and, to a degree, also in the United States) in the nineteenth century and in the first half of the twentieth. Both the White Paper and the *numerus clausus* originally triggered the cry of "never again," which constitutes a defining motif in the collective Zionist and Israeli ethos. So much for history. In the contemporary context, one of Israel's greatest and somewhat realistic fears is that the Arab population will eventually outnumber the Jewish population. This fear is one of the reasons for Israel's complete and almost automatic admission of all Jews and is believed by many people to justify the rejection of any proposal to change the Law of Return and Israel's immigration policies.

On a symbolic and emotional level, Jewish history provides significant reasons for not waiving the declaration in the Law of Return that "Every Jew has the right to immigrate to Israel." However, I doubt whether these reasons provide a sufficient justification for preferential immigration practices guided by the principle of "all Jews and only Jews." According to one of the principles for nationality-based preferences in immigration proposed above, the state constitutes a safe haven for all members of the national group that might be suffering from persecution. All of these group members should therefore be granted special immigration rights. The inclusion of this principle in the set of principles for nationality-based preferences in immigration renders any association of these principles with the 1939 White Paper totally groundless. The principles I have proposed also include the principle that, in the places where national groups have realized their self-determination, they are entitled to admit the number of members of their national diasporas required to maintain their right to national self-determination. This principle serves to respond to the well-founded demographic concerns of the Jews living in Israel.

5. OTHER MEANS FOR ACHIEVING DEMOGRAPHIC OBJECTIVES

The Law of Return and nationality-based preferences in immigration in general are ways of achieving the demographic goals of maintaining a majority or a population that is large enough to allow members of the group enjoying self-determination to continue living within their culture. The question that remains is whether additional steps could be taken to achieve these goals. In the introduction to this chapter, I mentioned the bill intended to encourage emigration to Arab countries, which was proposed to the 15th Knesset by Member of Knesset Michael Kleiner, but did not pass, and the amendment to the Citizenship Law, which was passed. This amendment denies Palestinian residents of the occupied territories and their Israeli family members the right to live together in Israel. The first two articles in Kleiner's bill stated the following: "1. A resident or citizen of Israel wishing to emigrate to an Arab country shall be entitled to special payment for that purpose; 2. Entitlement to such funds shall be contingent on waiving citizenship or permanent residence."[23] Kleiner explained his bill as fulfilling the need "to encourage the departure of citizens that do not identify with the Jewish character of the state and have an interest in emigrating from it." Though not stated explicitly in the explanatory note, Kleiner's bill was intended to reinforce Jewish demographic predominance

---

[23] See note 7 above.

in Israel by encouraging its Arab citizens to emigrate. Although Kleiner did not explicitly refer to Arabs in his bill, this was clearly his intention. The Knesset presidency therefore disqualified the bill by appealing to the appropriate section of the Knesset regulations which allow it to dismiss racist bills. As for the amendment to the Israeli Citizenship Law, which would deny the right of Palestinian residents of the occupied territories and relatives of theirs who have Israeli citizenship to family unification, this proposal was submitted by the government to the 16th Knesset and was passed by the 17th Knesset.[24] Many Knesset members protested against the bill, claiming that it was racist. In my discussion above, I rejected the criticism of the Law of Return as racist and argued that immigration priorities based on national affiliation are not necessarily racist. However, should this conclusion also apply to the law preventing the unification of Palestinian families and to Kleiner's bill? Could one not argue that discrimination against Arab citizens of Israel with regard to the realization of their right to family unification is based on the fact that it is Israeli Arabs and no other group in Israel that threaten the viability of Jewish self-determination in Israel, that the realization of this right is a legitimate aspiration, and that accordingly, if discrimination in favor of Jews with respect to immigration is a legitimate means of realizing this right, then it should be equally legitimate to discriminate in favor of the Jews with regard to the right of family unification? Addressing the issue of denying Palestinians the right to family unification, Ruth Gavison stated:

> [I]ts justification derives from the fact that it is part of the continued effort to preserve Israel as a state in which the Jewish people realizes its right to self-determination in view of the conditions and circumstances in this region at this time.... Anyone supporting the idea of a stable solution of two states for the two peoples cannot also demand that the Palestinians' right to family unification within the State of Israel be recognized. As a matter of principle, Palestinian families should be unified within the framework of their state and Jewish families should be unified in their own state.[25]

However, taking this position a step further, it could be argued that supporting "a stable solution of two states for the two peoples" also means denying the Palestinians a right to have children within the borders of Israel.

---

[24] See note 8 above.

[25] Ruth Gavison, "Unification of Families in Two States," *Yedioth Ahronoth* (August 5, 2003), 24 hours supplement, 11 (Hebrew).

In the spirit of Gavison's argument, one might maintain that both Palestinians and Jews should only give birth to children in their own respective states. If these are legitimate means of demographic regulation, then clearly the Kleiner bill is legitimate too. Kleiner may also have based his bill on the claim that the realization of Jewish self-determination is indeed threatened by Arabs and not by anyone else. Perhaps Kleiner thought that, if this goal justifies discrimination in favor of Jews with regard to immigration to Israel, then conceivably, the same goal could also justify using financial rewards to encourage Arabs to emigrate.

Are there nonetheless moral differences among Kleiner's bill, discrimination in favor of Jews with regard to immigration to Israel, and the restrictions on the rights of Israeli Palestinians to family unification? In my opinion, an answer is provided by the definition of the concept of "racial discrimination" in Article 1 of the UN International Convention on the Elimination of All Forms of Racial Discrimination, which I have already mentioned. Article 1 defines racism differently from the primary sense specified in section 1 of this chapter. According to the primary sense, distinctions between people are racist if they are applied based on membership in groups to which people belong by birth or upbringing and if these distinctions are invoked for purposes unrelated to the particular group membership. On the other hand, Article 1 states that racial discrimination applies to "*any* distinction, exclusion, restriction or preference based on race . . . or national or ethnic origin which has the purpose or *effect* of nullifying or impairing the recognition, enjoyment or exercise, on an equal footing, of human rights and fundamental freedoms" (italics mine). Under this definition, discrimination could be considered racist even if group membership is relevant for achieving a particular purpose. *Any* race- or origin-based distinction or restriction is racist if it has the purpose or even just *the effect* of impairing people's enjoyment of human rights on an equal footing. According to this criterion, the Knesset's decision to restrict the Palestinians' right of family unification would certainly be considered to be racism, because it forces them to only choose spouses who have the same citizenship as they do or to pay a heavy price for choosing Palestinian spouses from the occupied territories on the West Bank or the Gaza Strip. They must either live apart from their spouses or leave their homes in Israel. Unlike Gavison, who believes that the basic right to family life does not necessarily entail that the state must allow individuals to realize this right in the same place where they grew up or where their lives are established, I believe that the right to family life does entail a legal right to exercise it in the same place where a person's life is already firmly established.[26] But above all, it is a moral right, as binding as the right people have to give birth to children and to raise them in the same place where their lives are established, to acquire their education in the same place, to work there in order to earn a living, and to continue living there. These are basic human rights. They must be imposed as constraints on the demographic regulation measures adopted by states in order to promote the right to self-determination of ethnocultural groups.

Similarly, Kleiner's law must also be considered racist even though I believe it is somewhat less problematic than denying Palestinians the right to family unification. Subsidizing the emigration of Arab citizens of Israel is indeed intended to encourage them to leave. But ultimately, the question of whether or not they leave depends on them. The proposed subsidization does not impose any kind of restriction on the freedom of Israeli Arabs, nor does it deny them any freedom of action within any important sphere of their lives. It does not restrict their careers, their ability to acquire an education, or their mobility. Nor does it restrict their ability to marry or to raise a family. It also does not restrict their political freedom. However, subsidizing the emigration of Palestinians who are citizens of Israel is nonetheless illegitimate. By passing such a law, the state would in effect be saying to its Arab citizens that their ethnocultural identity renders them undesirable. Admittedly, the import of such a statement is more symbolic than practical. However, the message conveyed by such a law would be a particularly offensive one.[27] In the late 1960s, the Conservative MP Enoch Powell made a similar proposal with regard to British citizens who had originally immigrated to the United Kingdom from the West Indies. The proposal

---

[26] The European Convention on Human Rights seems to acknowledge such a right in Articles 8 and 10. According to Articles 8 and 10, it is possible for a government to limit this right. Nevertheless, I do not believe this applies to the case at hand.

[27] Since Kleiner's bill leaves the choice of whether or not to leave Israel in the hands of the Arabs themselves, it conceivably has no practical import because presumably there are not many Arabs who would take advantage of the subsidy offered by Kleiner. The amendment of the Citizenship Law, on the other hand, is certain to have practical consequences. As a result of the law, when an Arab man or woman who is an Israeli citizen marries a Palestinian from the West Bank or the Gaza Strip who is not an Israeli citizen, this will ultimately reduce the Israeli Arab population since the couple will be forced to leave Israel. Therefore, pragmatic considerations might well induce a racist MK to disqualify Kleiner's law, while simultaneously giving his support to the amendment of the Citizenship Law. Conceivably, this is the real explanation for the fact that the Knesset affirmed the denial of the rights for family unification and yet rejected Kleiner's law. In addition, Kleiner's notoriety as a racist is established to a degree which made all others want to dissociate themselves from him.

was condemned throughout Britain. And yet, Powell's proposal was perhaps slightly less problematic than Kleiner's proposal because it pertained to immigrant minorities as opposed to members of a homeland group, as was the case in Kleiner's proposal. If my arguments in earlier parts of this book are correct, the status of homeland groups in their homeland warrants even more protection than that of immigrant minorities.

Nationality-based priorities in immigration of the kind granted to Jews by the Law of Return—namely, privileges in immigration granted to members of ethnocultural groups in immigrating to the state where their group has realized its right to self-determination—differ from Kleiner's bill and from the issue of family unification for Palestinians. First, though the privileges in question are granted on the basis of ethnic, religious, or national origin, they do not result in a violation of human rights. Granting such priorities to Jews in Israel while failing to do so for Arabs does not result in their missing out on any important aspect of their lives, at least not directly or in any nonnegligible way. Second, these privileges can be granted equally to all ethnocultural groups, so that for each and every ethnocultural group, there is a state ruling its homeland or part thereof within which it enjoys these privileges. Under these circumstances, if an ethnocultural group enjoys special immigration privileges in one particular state in the world, then it would not be justified for members of the same group living in another country to consider such special immigration privileges offensive when they are awarded to another ethnocultural group. There is no doubt that the principal injustice caused by Israel's Law of Return does not stem from the fact that it grants advantages in immigration on the basis of nationality. Rather, it stems from the fact that it grants the advantages to one ethnocultural group within a state which also includes members of another ethnocultural group whose homeland it controls, but who are denied the same advantages. If the appropriate solution to the current stage of the Jewish-Palestinian conflict is really the establishment of two separate states, then it is only natural that Jews should have special immigration privileges in Israel while Palestinians would have similar immigration privileges in the other state. In contrast to the case of the denial of family unification rights, the realization of the Palestinians' right to immigration privileges in the Palestinian state and not in Israel does not involve the potential violation of important individual rights of Israeli Palestinians, such as the right to marry the person of their choice or the right to have a family. Instituting special immigration rights that are biased in favor of Jews in Israel while the Palestinians enjoy similar preferential treatment in another state therefore seems to be a legitimate means of demographic regulation intended to preserve demographic Jewish predominance in Israel or to maintain a population large enough to allow members of the group to continue living their lives within their own culture. In addition to special immigration privileges for Jews, the only legitimate means for achieving these goals that I can think of is a state policy that would encourage non-Jewish (and non-Arab) immigrants to Israel to integrate culturally and socially into the Jewish community rather than into the Arab community in Israel.[28] However, such a policy could only be adopted if immigration to Israel ceased to be limited to Jews. I find it hard to imagine any other legitimate legal means for achieving the demographic goals necessary for the existence of self-determination of ethnocultural groups.

6. HEGEMONY IN AREAS OTHER THAN DEMOGRAPHY

As noted above, Israel has not only applied the hegemonic interpretation of the Jewish right to self-determination to demographic issues. The principle of Jewish hegemony was accorded constitutional status in the basic laws of Israel. It is also realized in numerous laws and practices in the following areas: land acquisition, education, political participation, employment, resource allocation, legal interpretation, state symbols, compulsory military service, the national anthem, names of places and of state institutions, the main official language, and official holidays. In many areas, this is not only a matter of hegemony, but one of exclusivity. Only Jews are represented by state symbols such as the design of the Israeli flag, the text of the national anthem, names of various government institutions, and the name of the state itself. Detailed discussion of the appropriate arrangements in each of these fields is far beyond the scope of this book. However, it is important to note that, unlike the areas of demography and security, none of the arguments discussed for Jewish hegemony in Israel in chapter 3—that is, the arguments invoking the right to self-determination as such, the fact that many states perceive themselves as states belonging to one hegemonic ethnic nation, the Jews' long history of persecution, and the history of the conflict between Jews and Arabs—can justify Jewish hegemony in these fields, let alone exclusivity.

Maintaining a Jewish majority and Jewish military control do not justify inequality or discrimination in all areas that are not directly connected

---

[28] This resembles the requirement in Quebec according to which immigrants should educate their children in French rather than in English. See also note 15 above.

to security. They certainly do not justify budgetary or political discrimination. Specifically, they do not justify greater budgetary allocation per capita for the education of Jews than for the education of Arabs and the provision of more funds per capita for religious services for Jews compared to the funds allocated to religious services for Arabs. Nor can they justify hiring employees for public offices in a manner that discriminates against Arabs. Moreover, maintaining a majority and control over military forces certainly do not justify discrimination in land allocation and in the government's accommodation of Arab housing needs compared to those of Jews.[29] Indeed, the very need to make these remarks is embarrassing; they should be self-evident, and there should not be any need to spell them out explicitly. Unfortunately, this is not the case in the current social and legal climate in Israel.[30]

Maintaining a Jewish majority and Jewish military control also provide no justification for imposing restrictions on the right to political participation of the sort delineated in section 7A of the Knesset Elections Law and

---

[29] The Supreme Court ruling in *Ka'adan* (HCJ 6698/95, *Ka'adan v. Israel Land Administration*, P.D. 54[1], 258 [Hebrew]) was certainly a step in the right direction on this painful issue. The Court rejected the claim that the State of Israel's Jewishness justified the allocation of land for the establishment of exclusively Jewish settlements primarily in view of the fact that the State of Israel has consistently avoided allocating any land for the expansion of Arab towns or neighborhoods or for the establishment of new Arab towns and villages. However, the reality in Israel continues to be as described by Ruth Gavison's admonition: "It is unacceptable that in all of the years since the State was established hundreds of new Jewish villages have been established and not even one Arab village" (Ruth Gavison, *Can Israel Be Both Jewish and Democratic: Tensions and Prospects* [Jerusalem: Van Leer Institute, Hakibbutz Hameuchad, 1999], 113–114 [Hebrew]).

[30] See previous note. Another prominent example of this point can be found in HCJ 6924/98, *The Association for Civil Rights in Israel v. The Government of Israel*, P.D. 55(5), 15 (Hebrew), which dealt with Arab representation on the board of directors of the Israel Land Administration Council. This ruling is an application of the principle of equality in the allocation of resources, opportunities, and positions. Justice Yitzhak Zamir cited the legal sources forming the basis for the obligatory nature of this principle in Israeli law and a series of laws which implement it, including those that specifically mention the state's obligation to ensure that the Arab population is adequately represented in public service. He also defines what I believe to be the correct view of the concept of adequate representation: Its implementation depends on the specific nature of the body in which Arab representation is granted, "which includes the practical importance of the body from the point of view of the group entitled to appropriate representation." Furthermore, according to this principle, "the importance attributed to representation in the Board of Directors of the Israel Land Administration Council is greater with respect to the Arab population than it is for example with respect to people with disabilities" (paragraph 31 of the ruling). Similar remarks can be made with respect to the current situation pertaining to Arab representation in other branches of the civil service.

section 5 of the Parties Law, which do not allow political parties to register or participate in elections if they reject the Jewish character of the state. Admittedly, applying these instructions could clearly serve as means to preserve Jewish hegemony in Israel. However, the laws in question diametrically contradict basic democratic principles. The character and identity of democratic states are matters to be decided by the majority of the citizens or by a special majority. Blocking the way to change the character and identity of a state by denying any particular group the right to be elected and the right to persuade the majority or a special majority to support such change violates the principle of majority rule. As such, it is manifestly undemocratic and violates the right to political participation.[31] This is certainly the case when the law is used to limit the power of the majority in deciding highly controversial matters of political morality disputed by both the public at large and among political theorists. For example, according to the interpretation proposed in this book for the concept of a Jewish state, one should support the existence of a Jewish majority in Israel for reasons of security and not because a Jewish majority is inherent to the right to self-determination. According to Supreme Court rulings that interpreted section 7A and according to the prevalent position held by most Israeli Jews, the need to maintain a Jewish majority follows from the right to Jewish self-determination. This means that, by including the position for which I have been arguing in this book in its political platform, a political party would disqualify itself from the Knesset elections. This is of course manifestly antidemocratic. Even if it directly serves to promote Jewish hegemony in Israel, it contradicts and conflicts with basic political human rights. These rights should serve as constraints on the means that the state can legitimately use in order to promote a particular ethnocultural group's right to self-determination.

Jewish control of the armed forces and proactively maintaining a Jewish majority also do not justify the denial of collective rights to Arabs, such as autonomy in certain areas, parliamentary representation, and representation in the public domain. Consider the subject of autonomy in education. Except for general requirements that apply to all students irrespective of their cultural affiliation, which pertain to general knowledge and to civic values, nothing justifies denying the Arab population such autonomy. It is difficult to prove that a denial of this kind of autonomy to Arabs contributes anything to Jewish security in the long run. Therefore, it could hardly be

---

[31] See also Gavison, *Can Israel Be Both Jewish and Democratic*, 91.

considered a form of self-defense. It would seem that this denial of autonomy in education is likely to aggravate the relationship between Jews and
Arabs, which ultimately will create more security concerns.

The same applies to the general representation of the Arab population
in the public domain and in the symbols of the state. Their representation
should reflect the size of their population in the country as a whole and
in specific areas. In the year 2000, former state comptroller and Supreme
Court justice Miriam Ben-Porat, hardly someone who would have been
expected to hold radical political views, proposed adding a verse to the
national anthem, "Hatikvah," which would allow the Arab citizens of Israel
to identify with the state's exclusively Jewish national anthem. Her proposal was met with scathing criticism from those representing mainstream
Zionism.[32] They apparently assumed that, without Jewish exclusivity in the
signs and symbols of the state and its national anthem, the state would
cease to be a Jewish state and would no longer realize the Jewish right to
self-determination. However, given my interpretation of the right to self-
determination as presented in chapter 3, this view seems to be mistaken. As
argued in chapter 3, for as long as they retain their validity, Jewish security
concerns justify attempts to maintain a Jewish majority and Jewish control
over the military. However, these concerns are entirely unrelated to matters
such as representation in the public domain and in state symbols. As in the
case of denying Arabs autonomy in education, denying them the right to be
represented in the symbols of the state and in the public domain can hardly
be considered a form of self-defense and usually aggravates the situation,
which, as I noted above, ultimately creates more security concerns.[33]

In two cases dealing with the language rights of the Arab minority
in Israel, Israel's Supreme Court took a major step in the direction I have
proposed here. The first case (*Re'em Engineers*)[34] pertains to a petition to

---

[32] She made the proposal at a ceremony for the ordination of Reform rabbis in the
Hebrew Union College of Jerusalem. According to *Maariv* (September 15, 2000), which
reported the proposal, "Member of Knesset Rehavam Zeevi and the fifth President Yitzhak
Navon left the ceremony in protest."

[33] Denying Arabs any representation in state symbols is as alienating as denying them
autonomy in determining how their children should be educated. It constitutes unequal treatment similar to a differential allocation of financial resources among the two cultural groups.
Most Israeli Arab citizens have never accepted that they merit such discrimination. Therefore,
if such unequal treatment continues, this may well lead (this may already have led) to feelings
of resentment, which are ultimately incompatible with Jewish security interests.

[34] CA 105/92, *Re'em Engineers Ltd v. The Municipality of Nazareth Illit*, P.D. 47(5), 189
(Hebrew).

allow private commercial advertising exclusively in the language of a specific target audience. The specific case concerned an advertisement in Arabic for apartments in the Arab village of Yafia. The Supreme Court ruled that there was no justification for compelling the petitioners to add Hebrew to their advertisement. In the second case (*Adalah v. Tel Aviv–Yaffo Municipality*),[35] the Court ruled that in cities in which there is an Arab minority, the authorities were obligated to signpost the streets in Arabic and not just in Hebrew, since Arabs are an indigenous or homeland population in Israel.[36] However, I would like to emphasize that the Supreme Court did not go as far as it could have gone. In both rulings, the Court indicated that it could indeed rule in favor of Arabic, because the status of Hebrew was already secure, since it is the predominant language in Israel. However, the Court failed to explain why Hebrew should have such a status. There are several possible ways to justify this status. One is the fact that it is the language of the majority, which happens to be Hebrew-speaking. Another possible justification for this status is that it is entailed by the view that the right to self-determination entitles Jews to maintain a majority. Therefore, it follows indirectly that Hebrew must be the predominant language since it is the language of Israeli Jews. Finally, the special status of Hebrew could be directly justified by the Jews' right to self-determination, even if this right did not imply a right to form a majority. In my view, the predominance of Hebrew as the official language of the Jewish state is justified only because there actually is a Jewish majority in Israel. As explained above, however, this majority status should not be viewed as an implication of the right to self-determination as such. The interpretation of the right to self-determination presented here only entails a right to linguistic hegemony in those parts of

---

[35] HCJ 4112/99, *Adalah—The Legal Center for Arab Minority Rights in Israel v. The Municipality of Tel Aviv–Yaffo*, P.D. 56(5), 393 (Hebrew).

[36] The Supreme Court did not use these terms. Hedging the issue, it stated, "Arabic is the language of [the minority] . . . that has long been living in Israel" (paragraph 25 of the ruling by Chief Justice Aharon Barak). Similarly, the Supreme Court did not directly argue that the fact that Arabs are a homeland group should give them the right to have street signs in Arabic in cities in which they constitute a minority. The Supreme Court ruling invoked the legal status of Arabic as an official language under Article 82 of the King's Order in Council for Palestine, 1922–1947, which specifically requires street signs to also be in Arabic in those cities in which there is an Arab minority. This article is still in force in Israel. But it should be noted here that the importance of this ruling is not so much in the decision itself, as in the argument invoked by the majority judges (Chief Justice Aharon Barak and Justice Dalia Dorner), which verge on acknowledging collective rights for the Arab minority in Israel.

the state where the majority speaks the particular language of the group exercising self-determination. The right to self-determination does not require that the language of those enjoying linguistic predominance in particular geographical areas necessarily be the main language of the entire state. Nor does the right to self-determination as such require that those enjoying self-determination be a majority.

Conclusion

From the extreme ultranationalist Right to the very moderate Left, all of the different versions of Zionism share two common tenets: First, the Jews must realize and maintain their right to national self-determination, and second, this must be done in the Land of Israel. However, the versions of Zionism differ with regard to the institutional, demographic, and territorial dimensions of Jewish self-determination. In this book, I have invoked considerations of distributive justice and considerations of remedial justice in order to examine the desirable dimensions of Jewish self-determination in the Land of Israel in the past, present, and future.

In chapter 1, I argued that the historical developments between the 1880s and the late 1940s, which determined the details of the institutional, territorial, and demographic dimensions of the Zionist aspiration to realize Jewish self-determination in Palestine, also had normative consequences. While justifications for the Zionist aspiration did exist in the 1880s, at this point in time, any such justifications had not yet become incontrovertible. Historically, this is clearly reflected by the fact that there was a rivalry between Zionism and the Bund regarding the solution for "the Jewish problem," which neither side seemed to win. During the 1930s and 1940s, following the Nazi rise to power, the Arab revolt, and the Holocaust, the justifications for Zionism became indisputable. The fact that the justice of Zionism did not seem unquestionable until the 1930s meant that the Zionist movement had to be modest in its aspirations for Jewish self-determination in Palestine. And indeed such modesty was reflected in the ambitions actually voiced by the Zionist movement at that time. The Nazi rise to power in Germany and the rise of fascism in various parts of Europe, however, rendered the Zionist aspiration to establish a Jewish state in Palestine conclusively just. This was granted international recognition by the UN Resolution for the Partition of Palestine of November 1947. The Arab rejection of this resolution and the war which the Arab states subsequently launched against the Jewish community in Palestine further enhanced the justice of the establishment of the State of Israel.

However, Israel has since then deviated from the justifiable aspirations of Zionism. These deviations have been in the institutional, territorial, and demographic dimensions of Jewish self-determination. In 1948, although Israel fought a just war for its independence, a huge number of Palestinians became refugees. This wreaked havoc on Palestinian society. Since the 1967 Six-Day War, Israel has been establishing more and more Jewish settlements in the territories occupied in this war and has been oppressing the Palestinians living there. Moreover, in all of the years of its existence, Israel has interpreted its Jewishness as entitling the Jews to hegemony and even exclusivity in almost all spheres, especially those pertaining to public life.

It is important to realize that, if the moral theses developed in this book are correct, then the practical measures they entail must be implemented as soon as possible, not only because they are correct, but also because failure to do so will have negative repercussions for the future of the Jewish-Arab conflict. It is morally incumbent upon the parties to the conflict to terminate it as soon as possible. Israel's establishment of Jewish settlements in Palestinian territories beyond Israel's pre-1967 borders, as well as many of the discriminatory practices against Israeli Arabs within these borders, are justified neither by the Jews' right to self-determination nor by the nature and history of the Jewish-Arab conflict. As such, they constitute an additional source of frustration and rage for the Palestinians and for Israeli Arabs, and help to perpetuate the conflict. Admittedly, the resolution of the conflict also depends on the conduct of the Palestinians and their recognition of the justified right of Jews to national self-determination in a land which also happens to be their own homeland. Nonetheless, each party to the dispute is duty-bound to refrain from inflammatory and provocative practices that perpetuate the dispute and that cannot be regarded as being legitimate means of self-defense. The occupation and settlement activity beyond Israel's pre-1967 borders and the inequality between Jews and Arabs within these borders constitute such inflammatory or provocative practices.

Moreover, Israel must bring all of this to an end not only because the occupation of the West Bank and the inequality between Jews and Arabs in Israel are bad in and of themselves and corrupt Israel's present and future moral standing, but also because these practices render Israel's good faith in relying on the justice of Zionism's past questionable.

Let me explain this last point. According to the argument presented in chapter 2, the Jews' historical right to select the site for the realization of their self-determination in the Land of Israel ought to have been suspended since our non-ideal world lacks the appropriate institutions for specifying and enforcing the principles of ideal justice. However, due to the need to rescue themselves from persecution at the end of the nineteenth century and in the first half of the twentieth century, the Jews nevertheless had a remedial justification for realizing their primary right to self-determination and for determining its site in their historic homeland. As I explained in chapter 2, the basic rationale of the defense of necessity, which justifies acts that are normally prohibited, is that of the lesser evil. It is justifiable for a mortally wounded person to break into a pharmacy and steal medicines that will save his life, because the wrong which breaking into the pharmacy causes, namely, the damage to the pharmacy, is clearly a lesser evil than that which would result if he refrained from breaking into the pharmacy. Breaking into the pharmacy constitutes a lesser evil because the damage caused by the break-in is to property and not to life. Moreover, the break-in is a one-time event which does not create a permanent state of affairs. The damage is reversible since the owner of the pharmacy can easily be compensated for it. As emphasized in chapter 2, the Jews' return to Palestine is not such a clear-cut case. It was intended to save Jewish lives and restore Jewish dignity. However, the Jews couldn't just break in as it were for the purpose of picking up a particular kind of medicine and then leaving. They had to take possession of part of the pharmacy itself. To make things worse, Israel has taken possession of the whole pharmacy, and instead of being compensated, the pharmacist has been humiliated and oppressed. In order for the irreversible consequences of the Jews' return to be less damaging to the Palestinians, Israel should not have established settlements in the occupied territories, since they make it exceedingly difficult to terminate Israel's occupation of Palestinian territories. Also, Israel should have ended its discriminatory practices within the State of Israel long ago. Together with the countries of the world, and especially the European nations, Israel should have searched for ways to compensate the Palestinians for the price they have paid for the realization of Zionist ideology.

The fact that Israel has not stopped its policies of territorial expansion and discriminatory practices undermines its capacity to now invoke the necessity defense in good faith. As I hope I have shown, and as many early Zionist leaders, such as Pinsker, Herzl, Weizmann, Jabotinsky, and Ben-Gurion also believed, this defense is crucial for the justification of Zionism.

In this sense, the State of Israel's current actions and policies do not only undermine its moral standing in the present and in the future. They also affect the legitimacy of relying on the justice of the Zionist past. For someone like myself, whose life has to a great extent been shaped by Zionism and who wholeheartedly believes in the moral possibility of a just Zionism, this is indeed tragic.

Bibliography

Agassi, Joseph. *Liberal Nationalism for Israel: Towards an Israeli National Identity.* Jerusalem: Gefen, 1999.

Ahad Ha'am. "Three Steps." *The Writings of Ahad Ha'am,* 150–153. Tel Aviv: Dvir, 1947. (Hebrew.)

Almog, Shmuel. *Zionism and History: The Rise of a New Jewish Consciousness.* New York: St. Martin's, 1987.

Anderson, Benedict. *Imagined Communities: Reflections on the Origin and Spread of Nationalism,* rev. ed. London: Verso, 1991.

Avizohar, Meir, and Isaiah Friedman, eds. *Studies in the Palestine Partition Plans, 1937–1947.* Sede Boqer: Ben-Gurion Research Center, 1984. (Hebrew.)

Avnery, Uri. *War or Peace in the Semitic World.* Tel Aviv: Young Palestine Association, 1947. (Hebrew.)

Avni, Haim. *Argentina: "The Promised Land": Baron De Hirsch's Colonization Project in the Argentine Republic.* Jerusalem: Magnes, 1973. (Hebrew.)

Avni, Haim, and Gideon Shimoni, eds. *Zionism and Its Jewish Opponents.* Jerusalem: Hassifriya Haziyonit, 1990. (Hebrew.)

Barry, Brian. *Culture and Equality: An Egalitarian Critique of Multiculturalism.* Cambridge: Polity, 2001.

Bartlett, Richard H. "Native Title in Australia: Denial, Recognition, and Dispossession." In Paul Haveman, ed., *Indigenous Peoples' Rights in Australia, Canada, and New Zealand,* 408–427. Auckland: Oxford University Press, 1999.

Barzilay-Yegar, Dvorah. *A National Home for the Jewish People: The Concept in British Political Thinking and Policy Making, 1917–1923.* Jerusalem: Hassifriaya Haziyonit, 2003. (Hebrew.)

Ben-Israel, Hedva. *In the Name of the Nation: Studies in Nationalism and Zionism.* Jerusalem: Ben-Gurion University of the Negev Press, 2004. (Hebrew.)

Benjamini, Eliahu. *States for the Jews: Uganda, Birobidzhan and 34 Other Projects.* Tel Aviv: Hakibbutz Hameuchad, 1990. (Hebrew.)

Ben-Ze'ev, Efrat. "The Politics of Taste and Smell: Palestinian Rites of Return." *Alpayim* 25 (2003), 73–88. (Hebrew.)

Berlin, Isaiah. "Nationalism: Past Neglect and Present Power." In Isaiah Berlin, *Against the Current: Essays in the History of Ideas,* ed. Henry Hardy, 333–355. New York: Viking, 1980.

Blatman, Daniel. "The Bund: The Myth of Revolution and the Reality of Every-day Life." In Israel Bartal and Israel Guttman, eds., *The Broken Chain: Polish Jewry through the Ages*, vol. 2, 493–533. Jerusalem: Zalman Shazar Center, 2001. (Hebrew.)

———. *For Our Freedom and Yours: The Jewish Labor Bund in Poland, 1939–1949*. London: Valentine Mitchell, 2003.

Buchanan, Allen. *Justice, Legitimacy and Self-Determination: Moral Foundations for International Law*. New York: Oxford University Press, 2004.

Carens, Joseph H. "Aliens and Citizens: The Case for Open Borders." *Review of Politics* 49 (1987), 251–273.

Conforti, Yitzhak. *Past Tense: Zionist Historiography and the Shaping of the National Memory*. Jerusalem: Yad Izhak Ben-Zvi, 2006. (Hebrew.)

Diamond, James S. *Homeland or Holy Land? The "Canaanite" Critique of Israel*. Bloomington: Indiana University Press, 1986.

Dothan, Shmuel. *Partition of Eretz-Israel in the Mandatory Period: The Jewish Controversy*. Jerusalem: Yad Izhak Ben-Zvi, 1979. (Hebrew.)

Dressler, Joshua. "New Thoughts about the Concept of Justification in the Criminal Law: A Critique of Fletcher's Thinking and *Rethinking*." *UCLA Law Review* 32 (1984), 61–69.

Evron, Boas. *A National Reckoning*, 2nd ed. Or Yahuda: Dvir, 2002. (Hebrew.)

Fletcher, George. *Rethinking Criminal Law*. Boston: Little, Brown, 1978.

Friedman, Isaiah. "Herzl and the Uganda Controversy." *Iyunim Bitkumat Israel* 4 (1994), 175–203. (Hebrew.)

Gafni [Weinshenker], Reuven. *Our Historical-Legal Right to Eretz Israel*. Jerusalem: Sifriyat Torah ve-Avoda, 1933. (Hebrew.)

Galnoor, Itzhak. *Territorial Partition: Decision Crossroads in the Zionist Movement*. Jerusalem: Magnes, 1994. (Hebrew.)

Gans, Chaim. "Historical Rights." *Mishpatim* 21 (1992), 193–220. (Hebrew.)

———. *The Limits of Nationalism*. Cambridge: Cambridge University Press, 2003.

Gavison, Ruth. "The Jews' Right to Statehood: A Defense." *Azure* 15 (2003), 70–108.

———. *Can Israel Be Both Jewish and Democratic? Tensions and Prospects*. Jerusalem: Van Leer Institute, Hakibbutz Hameuchad, 1999. (Hebrew.)

Gellner, Ernest. *Nations and Nationalism*. Oxford: Basil Blackwell, 1983.

Gorny, Yosef. *Converging Alternatives: The Bund and the Zionist Labor Movement, 1897–1985*. Albany: State University of New York Press, 2006.

———. *Policy and Imagination: Federal Ideas in Zionist Political Thought, 1917–1948*. Jerusalem: Yad Izhak Ben-Zvi, Hassifriya Haziyonit, 1993. (Hebrew.)

———. *The State of Israel in Jewish Public Thought: The Quest for Collective Identity*. New York: New York University Press, 1994.

———. *Zionism and the Arabs, 1882–1948: A Study of Ideology*, trans. Chaya Galai. Oxford: Clarendon, 1987.

Habermas, Jürgen. "Recognition and Redistribution: What Does It Take to Reproduce a Culture." *Tel Aviv University Law Review* 27 (2003), 11–21. (Hebrew.)

Halpern, Ben. *The Idea of the Jewish State*, 2nd ed. Cambridge, MA: Harvard University Press, 1969.

Harel, Alon. "Whose Home Is It? Reflections on the Palestinians' Interest in Return." *Theoretical Inquiries in Law* 5 (2004), 333–366.

Hart, H. L. A. "Are There Any Natural Rights?" In Jeremy Waldron, ed., *Theories of Rights*, 77–90. New York: Oxford University Press, 1984.

Haveman, Paul, ed. *Indigenous Peoples' Rights in Australia, Canada, and New Zealand*. Auckland: Oxford University Press, 1999.

Hayden, Robert M. "Constitutional Nationalism in the Formerly Yugoslav Republics." *Slavic Review* 5 (1992), 654–673.

Hazony, Yoram. "Did Herzl Want a 'Jewish' State?" *Azure* 9 (2000), 37–73.

Heller, Joseph. *The Zionist Idea*. London: Joint Zionist Publications Committee, 1947.

Herzl, Theodor. *Altneuland*, trans. Lotta Levensohn. New York: Bloch, 1941.

———. *The Jewish State*, trans. Sylvie d'Avigdor. New York: Dover, 1988.

Hobbes, Thomas. *Leviathan*. Oxford: A. R. Mowbray & Co., 1946.

Hobsbawm, Eric J. *Nations and Nationalism since 1780*, 2nd ed. Cambridge: Cambridge University Press, 1992.

Horon, A. G. *The Land of Kedem: A Historical and Political Guide to the Near East*. Tel Aviv: Chermon, 1970. (Hebrew.)

Ignatieff, Michael. *Blood and Belonging: Journeys into the New Nationalism*. New York: Noonday, 1993.

Ivison, Duncan, Paul Patton, and Will Sanders, eds. *Political Theory and the Rights of Indigenous Peoples*. Cambridge: Cambridge University Press, 2000.

Kant, Immanuel. *The Metaphysical Elements of Justice*, trans. John Ladd. Indianapolis: Bobbs-Merrill, 1965.

Kaplan, Eran. "A Rebel with a Cause: Hillel Kook, Begin and Jabotinsky's Ideological Legacy." *Israel Studies* 10, no. 3 (2005), 87–103.

Kasher, Asa. "Justice and Affirmative Action: Naturalization and the Law of Return." *Israel Yearbook on Human Rights* 15 (1985), 101–112.

Kaufmann, Yechezkel. *Exile and Foreign Land*. Tel Aviv: Dvir, 1930. (Hebrew.)

Kohn, Hans, ed. *Nationalism and the Jewish Ethic: Basic Writings of Ahad Ha'am*. New York: Schocken, 1962.

———. *Nationalism: Its Meaning and History*. Princeton, NJ: Van Nostrand, 1955.

Kolatt, Israel. "Eretz Yisrael as a Focus of Dissent and Agreement between Zionists and Anti-Zionists." In Haim Avni and Gideon Shimoni, eds., *Zionism and Its Jewish Opponents*, 21–47. Jerusalem: Hassifriya Haziyonit, 1990. (Hebrew.)

Kymlicka, Will. "Western Political Theory and Ethnic Relations in Eastern Europe." In Will Kymlicka and Magda Opalski, eds., *Can Liberal Pluralism Be Exported? Western Political Theory and Ethnic Relations in Eastern Europe*, 13–106. Oxford: Oxford University Press, 2001.

———. *Liberalism, Community and Culture*. Oxford: Clarendon, 1989.

———. *Multicultural Citizenship: A Liberal Theory of Minority Rights*. Oxford: Clarendon, 1995.

Laqueur, Walter. *A History of Zionism*. New York: Schocken, 1976.

Laskov, Shulamit. "Altneuland." *Zionism* 15 (1990), 35–53. (Hebrew.)

Lyons, David. "The New Indian Claims and Original Rights to Land." In Jeffrey Paul, ed., *Reading Nozick: Essays on Anarchy, State and Utopia*, 355–379. Oxford: Basil Blackwell, 1982.

Marmor, Andrei. "Entitlement to Land and the Right of Return: An Embarrassing Challenge for Liberal Zionism." In Lukas H. Meyer, ed., *Justice in Time: Responding to Historical Injustice*, 319–333. Baden-Baden: Nomos, 2004.

Mill, John Stuart. "Representative Government." In John Stuart Mill, *Utilitarianism; On Liberty; Considerations on Representative Government; Remarks on Bentham's Philosophy*, ed. Geraint Williams, chap. 16. London: Dent, 1993.

Miller, David. *On Nationality*. Oxford: Clarendon, 1995.

Moore, Margaret. "The Territorial Dimension of Self-Determination." In Margaret Moore, ed., *National Self-Determination and Secession*, 134–157. Oxford: Oxford University Press, 1998.

——. *The Ethics of Nationalism*. Oxford: Oxford University Press, 2001.

Morris, Benny. "The New Historiography: Israel Confronts Its Past." *Tikkun* 3, no. 6 (1988), 19–23, 99–102.

——. *Israel's Border Wars, 1949–1956: Arab Infiltration, Israeli Retaliation and the Countdown to the Suez War*. Oxford: Oxford University Press, 1997.

——. *Righteous Victims: A History of the Zionist-Arab Conflict, 1881–2001*. New York: Vintage, 2001.

——. *The Birth of the Palestinian Refugee Problem, 1947–1949*. Cambridge: Cambridge University Press, 1987.

Nimni, Ephraim. *Marxism and Nationalism*. London: Pluto, 1991.

Pappé, Ilan. *Britain and the Arab-Israeli Conflict, 1948–51*. New York: St. Martin's, 1988.

Peled, Yoav. *Class and Ethnicity in the Pale: The Political Economy of Jewish Workers' Nationalism in Late Imperial Russia*. New York: St. Martin's, 1989.

Pfaff, William. *The Wrath of Nations: Civilization and the Furies of Nationalism*. New York: Simon & Schuster, 1993.

Pinsker, Leo. *Autoemancipation: An Appeal to His People*. New York: ZOA, 1948.

Poole, Ross. *Nation and Identity*. London: Routledge, 1999.

Ram, Uri. *The Time of the "Post": Nationalism and the Politics of Knowledge in Israel*. Tel Aviv: Resling, 2006. (Hebrew.)

Rawls, John. *A Theory of Justice*. Cambridge, MA: Harvard University Press, 1971.

Raz, Joseph. *The Morality of Freedom*. Oxford: Oxford University Press, 1986.

Raz, Joseph, and Avishai Margalit. "National Self-Determination." In Joseph Raz, *Ethics in the Public Domain: Essays in the Morality of Law and Politics*, rev. ed., 125–145. Oxford: Clarendon, 1994.

Renan, Ernest. "Qu'est-ce qu'une nation?" In John Hutchinson and Anthony D. Smith, eds., *Nationalism*, 17–18. Oxford: Oxford University Press, 1994.

Rousseau, Jean-Jacques. *The Social Contract*. London: J. M. Dent & Sons, 1920.

Seymour, Michel, with the collaboration of Jocelyne Couture and Kai Nielsen. "Introduction: Questioning the Ethnic/Civic Dichotomy." In Jocelyne Couture, Kai Nielsen, and Michel Seymour, eds., *Rethinking Nationalism*, 1–61. Calgary: University of Calgary Press, 1998.

Shapira, Anita. *Land and Power: The Zionist Resort to Force, 1881–1948*, trans. William Templer. New York: Oxford University Press, 1992.

Sharp, Andrew. *Justice and the Māori: The Philosophy and Practice of Māori Claims in New Zealand since the 1970s*, 2nd ed. Auckland: Oxford University Press, 1997.

Shavit, Yaakov. *The New Hebrew Nation: A Study in Israeli Heresy and Fantasy*. London: Frank Cass, 1987.

Shimoni, Gideon. *The Zionist Ideology*. Hanover, NH: Brandeis University Press, 1995.

———. *The Zionist Ideology*, trans. Smadar Milo. Jerusalem: Magnes, 2001. (Hebrew.)

Shlaim, Avi. *Collusion across the Jordan: King Abdullah, the Zionist Movement, and the Partition of Palestine*. New York: Columbia University Press, 1988.

Simmons, John A. "Historical Rights and Fair Shares." *Law and Philosophy* 14 (1995), 149–184.

Steinberg, Isaak Nachman. "Territorialism: Free Israel and 'Freeland.'" In Feliks Gross and Basil J. Vlavianos, eds., *Struggle for Tomorrow: Modern Political Ideologies of the Jewish People*, 112–129. New York: Arts, Inc., 1954.

Tamir, Yael. *Liberal Nationalism*. Princeton, NJ: Princeton University Press, 1993.

Taylor, Charles. "The Politics of Recognition." In A. Gutmann, ed., *Multiculturalism: Examining the Politics of Recognition*, 25–73. Princeton, NJ: Princeton University Press, 1994.

Waldron, Jeremy. "Minority Cultures and the Cosmopolitan Alternative." *University of Michigan Journal of Law Reform* 25 (1991–1992), 751–793.

———. "Settlement, Return and the Supersession Thesis." *Theoretical Inquiries in Law* 5 (2004), 237–268.

———. "Superseding Historic Injustice." *Ethics* 103 (1992), 4–28.

Walzer, Michael. *Spheres of Justice*. Oxford: Blackwell, 1983.

Webber, Jeremy. "Beyond Regret: Mabo's Implications for Australian Constitutionalism." In Duncan Ivison, Paul Patton, and Will Sanders, eds., *Political Theory and the Rights of Indigenous Peoples*, 60–88. Cambridge: Cambridge University Press, 2000.

Yakobson, Alexander, and Amnon Rubinstein. *Israel and the Family of Nations: Jewish Nation-State and Human Rights*. Tel Aviv: Schocken, 2003. (Hebrew.)

Yehoshua, A. B. "An Attempt to Identify and Understand the Foundations of Anti-Semitism." *Alpayim* 28 (2005), 11–30 (Hebrew).

———. "Between Right and Right: One Right and Another." In A. B. Yehoshua, *Between Right and Right*, trans. Arnold Schwartz, 75–106. Garden City, NY: Doubleday, 1981.

———. "The *Golah*: The Neurotic Solution." In A. B. Yehoshua, *Between Right and Right*, trans. Arnold Schwartz, 21–74. Garden City, NY: Doubleday, 1981.

Yuval, Israel J. "The Myth of the Jewish Exile from the Land of Israel." *Common Knowledge* 12, no. 1 (2006), 16–33.

Zangwill, Israel. "The Return to Palestine." *New Liberal Review* 2 (December 1901), 615–631.

Zerubavel, Yael. *Recovered Roots: Collective Memory and the Making of Israeli National Tradition*. Chicago: University of Chicago Press, 1995.

Zipperstein, Steven J. *Elusive Prophet: Ahad Ha'am and the Origins of Zionism.* Los Angeles: University of California Press, 1993.

LEGAL CASES

Israel

HCJ 265/87 *Beresford v. The Ministry of Interior,* P.D. 43(4) 793 (Hebrew).

EA 1/88 *Neiman v. Chairman of the Central Elections Committee for the Twelfth Knesset,* P.D. 42(4) 177 (Hebrew).

EA 2/88 *Ben Shalom v. The Central Elections Committee for the Twelfth Knesset,* P.D. 43(4) 221 (Hebrew).

CA 105/92 *Re'em Engineers Ltd v. The Municipality of Nazareth Elite,* P.D. 47(5) 189 (Hebrew).

HCJ 6698/95 *Ka'adan v. Israel Land Administration,* P.D. 54(1) 258 (Hebrew).

HCJ 6924/98 *The Association for Civil Rights in Israel v. The Government of Israel,* P.D. 55(5) 15 (Hebrew).

HCJ 4112/99 *Adalah—The Legal Center for Arab Minority Rights in Israel v. The Municipality of Tel Aviv–Yaffo,* P.D. 56(5) 393 (Hebrew).

HCJ 7052/03 *Adalah—The Legal Center for Arab Minority Rights in Israel v. The Minister of Interior.* Not yet published. (Hebrew.)

HCJ 11286/03 *Uzi Ornan et al. v. The Minister of Interior.* Not published. (Hebrew.)

Australia

Mabo v. Queensland. no. 2 (1992). 175 CLR1.

Canada

Delgamuukw v. British Columbia (1997). 153 DLR. 4th 193. SCC.

LEGISLATION

Israel

Israel's Declaration of Independence, Official Gazette 1, Tel Aviv. May 14, 1948.

Basic Law: The Knesset.

The Law of Return, 5710–1950.

Immunity of Members of Parliament Law. (Rights and Duties), 5711–1951.

The Citizenship Law, 5712–1952.

A Bill to Encourage Emigration to Arab States, 5761–2001.

The Citizenship and Entry into Israel Law. (Temporary Provision), 5763–2003.

NEWSPAPER ARTICLES

Bana, Jalal, and Uria Shavit. "The Palestinian Dream, the Israeli Nightmare." *Ha'aretz.* July 6, 2001. (Hebrew.)

Gavison, Ruth. "Unification of Families in Two States." *Yedioth Ahronoth.* August 5, 2003, 24 Hours supplement, 11. (Hebrew.)

Lam, Amira. "Let It Be Bad." *Yedioth Ahronoth.* December 6, 2002, Seven Days weekend magazine, 28. (Hebrew.)

Nurmela, Emma. "Repaying the Debt of Honor: Ingrian Immigration to Finland" (2003), available at: http://www.uta.fi/FAST/FIN/HIST/en-ingim. html (accessed 03/23/2008).

Walzer, Michael. Review of Noam Chomsky's *Peace in the Middle East? New York Times Book Review.* October 6, 1974, 6.

————. Letter to the editor, *New York Review of Books.* December 4, 2003, 57.

Yehoshua, A. B. "The Third Way." *Ha'aretz*, November 19, 1993, B5. (Hebrew.)

Zand, Shlomo, and Nir Baram. "The Zionist Quintet's Anxiety." *Ma'ariv.* May 9, 2005 (Hebrew), available at: http://www.nrg.co.il/online/1/ART/931/970. html (accessed 03/23/2008).

Index